MYSTERIES IN MY HANDS

MYSTERIES IN MY HANDS

Young People, Life, and the Rosary

Maureen P. Provencher

Saint Mary's Press™

Genuine recycled paper with 10% post-consumer waste. Printed with soy-based ink. 5087800

The publishing team included Barbara A. Murray, development editor; Lorraine Kilmartin, reviewer; Mary M. Bambenek, development administrator; Mary Koehler, permissions editor; Laurie Berg-Shaner, copy editor; Lynn Riska, typesetter; Kimberly K. Sonnek, designer and illustrator; Andy Palmer, art director; manufacturing coordinated by the production services department of Saint Mary's Press.

Jonathan Thomas Goebel, cover photo

Printed in the United States of America

Printing: 9 8 7 6 5 4 3 2 1

Year: 2013 12 11 10 09 08 07 06 05

ISBN 0-88489-832-6

Library of Congress Cataloging-in-Publication Data

Provencher, Maureen P.
    Mysteries in My Hands : young people, life, and the rosary / Maureen P. Provencher.
        p. cm.
    ISBN 0-88489-832-6 (pbk.)
        1. Rosary. 2. Teenagers—Religious life. I. Title.
BX2310.R7P76 2004
242'.74—dc22
                                                        2004013438

Contributing Authors:

Andrew Adams
Matthew Adams
Robin Adams
Katie Barnett
Hannah (Corey) Beaver
John P. Campbell
Justine Noel Coyne
Ashton D. Cozzo
Virginia Deaton
Carolyn Della Pietra
Liza Desranleau
Cristina Marie Garcia del Busto
Christopher Gosselin
Katelyn Gurley
Carla Anne Hernandez
Margaret Jumonville
Amanda Konrad
Faye LaRochelle
Joan LaRochelle
Kathleen Massey
Carolyn Pippen
Emily Ryan
Elysha Schickel

I dedicate this book to the memory of my grandmother, my Mémère, Marie-Jeanne Custeau McAuliffe, a woman of great strength, faith, and witness. Thank you, Mé, for having given me a glimpse of holiness through the suffering and joy of such an ordinary life as your own.

CONTENTS

PREFACE   10

CHAPTER 1
Introduction to the Rosary   12

CHAPTER 2
The Joyful Mysteries   32

CHAPTER 3
The Luminous Mysteries (The Mysteries of Light)   46

CHAPTER 4
The Sorrowful Mysteries   59

CHAPTER 5
The Glorious Mysteries   72

ACKNOWLEDGMENTS   87

Author Acknowledgments

I wish to thank, first and foremost, my family—my parents and grand-parents, who instilled in me a faith that sustains me; and my siblings, Brian, Keith, and Patrice—with whom I have shared the many myster-ies of our own lives.

In a special way, I thank my friends who offered their support and expertise for the development of this book: Fr. Jean-Paul Labrie, who offered me access to his personal library; Fr. Marc Bishop, who is a constant sounding board for me and my thoughts, most especially in breaking open the mysteries and developing questions to evoke witness stories from young people; the Adamses, all seven of them: Robin and Phil, Matthew, Andrew, Michael, Allie, and Christopher, for their constant love, prayerful support, and the comfort of their home when I needed a break or some inspiration.

Thanks to my editor, Barbara Murray, for believing in me.

Thanks to the many young people who dared to share a bit of themselves in connecting the mysteries of the rosary to our lives, and to the adults who shared with us their own experiences of the rosary.

Thanks to all ministers of youth, especially those who circulated the questions to youth and encouraged them to write. May God's blessing forever shine on you as builders of the Kingdom with the young. Because of your work and ministry, our Church is enriched.

Thanks to the faith communities in Maine, Vermont, and Massa-chusetts who have journeyed with me and helped form me in my becoming.

Thanks to Mary, mother of God, and to the Holy Spirit, who have had a hand in this from the beginning. Thank you for your inspiration in sharing the Good News through this effort. Thank you, Mary, for your constant intercession for me and for all your children. Pray for us, that we may be made worthy of the promises of Christ and grow in holiness, according to the will of the Father, like you.

PREFACE

My earliest memories of the rosary are those attached to my maternal grandmother. When I am quiet, I can still hear the whispers of such familiar words, powerful words of heartfelt prayer that became the background music of my childhood: *"Je vous salue Marie, pleine de grace, le Seigneur est avec vous . . ."* These were the words Mémère prayed every day of her life, three times a day, in joyful succession and in accompaniment to her daily routine. She usually prayed the first rosary of the day while folding laundry, the second during the evening hours, long after dinner, and the third at bedtime—the last, most important task of her day. Whenever I spent an overnight with her, these were the words that lulled me to sleep. They were words of comfort and peace, and they are, now, the words that continue to connect me with my grandmother, as her human life has ended. For her, not only was the rosary her prayer, it was the rhythm of her life.

I used to think, "Why pray to Mary when one can 'go direct' to Jesus," but I remembered my grandmother's relationship with Mary and devotion to her. I figured there must be something to a relationship with Mary because it was of such importance and great value to Mémère. Because I trusted her wholeheartedly, I decided to follow her lead. Eventually I made an attempt at beginning such a relationship, not knowing quite how to approach the mother of God! However, with time and patience, I have come to connect with this woman in a very real way, through her youthfulness and her wisdom and as a mother—so eager to share her joy, her Jesus, with me.

To Mary, a mere teenager, was revealed a long-awaited promise: the coming of the Messiah to whom she would give birth—a young woman to give flesh to the divine! It has always amazed me how God has revealed so much to the young and has depended so greatly on them throughout all salvation history. If God called the young then, I have no doubt that God is calling the young now, in our present age.

Mary can show us how best to trust and surrender to a God who calls us into relationship, to say "Yes!" with all that we are—with all our wonderfulness and all our sinfulness.

For me Mary has more relevance than ever before. It is she who, through this ancient of prayers, the rosary, leads us to a more intimate friendship with her son, the one we so desperately long to reach out for and find in our prayer. She accomplishes this through an invitation to journey with her through the mysteries of the rosary—her own memories of her son's life. It is this life in which we are led to witness and participate; a life that is all so intricately intertwined with her own, and likewise with ours if we desire it. It is Mary who witnesses to us, through her life, how to live as a disciple of the Lord.

As we journey together through the beginnings of the rosary and all the elements of this ageless prayer, my desire for you is to come to know Mary as real, not as one who is distant and intangible but as one who is teacher and mother of us all. I pray that I may be like my grandmother in passing on the faith and in leading you to a deeper understanding and experience of the rosary and a relationship with Jesus and his mother, our mother.

Let us pray for the intercession of Mary, through this most sacred and ordinary of prayers, to unite us to the one rhythm of all our lives, the fruit of her womb, Jesus.

CHAPTER 1

Introduction to the Rosary

What Is the Rosary?

> The rosary is a method, an instrument, of prayer. It was given to us by God through the Church to help us to pray. (M. Basil Pennington, *Praying by Hand*, page 33)

For many of us, when we first consider the rosary, our attention is automatically drawn to the repetitious hum of Hail Marys. For some it is an inviting, peaceful rhythm; but if you're anything like I was in my teens, I found it boring and monotonous, and I didn't understand why we needed to pray to Mary when we could go directly to Jesus.

Fortunately, in my pursuit to understand this prayer better, I've come to appreciate and even long for the repetitious rhythm. I know that is quite a change. My hope is that as we delve into this prayer together, you, too, will come to have a better understanding of the rosary—all its prayers, its methods, its rhythm, and the blessings that flow from it. What I've come to learn is that the rosary is so much more than what we may perceive it to be when we first look at it. So without further delay, let's begin with the rosary's origins and see why this prayer continues to be so popular. There's got to be a good reason for it!

Where Does It Come From?

There really isn't one point of origin for the rosary. Instead, this prayer has evolved over many centuries into what it is today. The rosary became an important part of our tradition for many reasons. We'll take a look at some of the influences that helped this prayer grow in popularity.

Saint Dominic

The story of the rosary begins with a missionary priest named Dominic, who later was named a saint. Dominic founded an order of preachers known as the Dominicans. The Dominicans are responsible for spreading the prayer of the rosary throughout the world. They adopted many of the elements of monastic life; however, rather than focusing on manual labor, their ministry was preaching the word of God. Today many parishes invite Dominican preachers to lead parish mission retreats and such.

Around the year 1221, it is believed that the Blessed Virgin appeared to Dominic in a dream, giving him the rosary as a powerful tool to convert the Albigenses in the region of Toulouse, France. The Albigenses followed the teachings of the Cathari, a people who did not believe that Jesus was a real man born of a real woman. They believed only in his divinity. Dominic was having a tough time trying to convert the Albigenses, and it seemed like a hopeless cause. That's when Mary stepped in. Dominic spent three days fasting and in prayer, the only thing left for him to do. Mary appeared to him and told him that an intellectual approach would not work in trying to convert the Albigenses, but that a practical approach would. She presented this early form of the rosary to the people as a remedy for sickness, because many of the people suffered from severe illnesses. It caught on, and as the people prayed Mary's prayer and heard of Dominic's apparition of the Virgin, more and more were converted to Catholicism.

Monastic Roots

The rosary is rooted in the liturgical prayer of the Church. In the medieval period, the desire was to give the laity (members of the Church who are not ordained) a form of common prayer. The monks focused on the Psalter (reciting the 150 psalms of the Old Testament). Because common folk could not read or afford a psalter, they recited the Lord's Prayer 150 times throughout the day. This became known as the "poor man's breviary." Eventually the laity were given beads, specifically to help them count their prayers.

As time went on, the monks adapted the angel Gabriel's greeting in Luke 1:28 to, "Hail, Mary, full of grace," adding this refrain to complete their prayer. Devotion to Mary grew rapidly, and some of the laity of the time replaced the Lord's Prayer with the Hail Mary, praying 150 of them on their beads.

The Hail Mary

Elizabeth's greeting to Mary at the Visitation (see Luke 1:42) was added to the monks' adaptation of the angel Gabriel's greeting, and the recitation of these two greetings became a great prayer of praise to God, in praise of Christ—the very purpose of both greetings. It wasn't until the thirteenth century that the name *Jesus* was added to complete it. By the fifteenth century, the 150 Hail Marys were organized into sets of ten, called decades, and included the Lord's Prayer at the beginning of each set.

The Mysteries

The mysteries are glimpses into the life of Christ and were originally divided into three sets, or types: the joyful (relating to the events surrounding Jesus's birth), the sorrowful (relating to Jesus's Passion and death), and the glorious (relating to Resurrection, not only for Jesus but for his mother as well). In 2002 Pope John Paul II added a new set of mysteries, which come directly from the Scriptures and are related to Jesus's public ministry, spanning the time between his baptism in the Jordan River and his Transfiguration. This new set, called the luminous mysteries, or mysteries of light, fill the gap between Jesus's childhood and his Passion.

How We Pray the Rosary

When I was growing up, one of my favorite things to do was to pull out the family pictures and bring back the memories, into the moment. I have great memories of my brother, Brian, and me pulling open the file cabinet drawers that contained all our pictures through the years and sprawling them out all over our parents' king-sized bed. Those pictures were priceless—some would make us burst into outright belly laughs, and, no matter how hard we would try to fight it, we'd never be able to get past a few others without tear-filled eyes, welled up by the pain still deep within from missing someone whose life affected us. The pictures helped us, then and now, to remember the times of joy in our lives, the times of growth, pain, and triumphant glory.

Jesus's life was no different. Although cameras were far from being invented when Jesus was growing up, the people of his time used storytelling and song to remember, and they had the Scriptures, just as we do today. The "pictures" of the rosary tell us Jesus's story in what we call the mysteries.

The Joyful Mysteries

The first of the four sets, or types, of mysteries is the joyful mysteries. This set of five mysteries focuses on Jesus's life from conception, when the angel Gabriel appeared to Mary announcing that she was to be the mother of God, to the age of twelve, when Mary and Joseph had been in Jerusalem for the festival of Passover and discovered, after a full day's travel, that Jesus was not with them. Even Jesus began to show some independence in his adolescence! The joyful mysteries focus on the joy of the Incarnation—God becoming human, becoming one of us.

The Luminous Mysteries (The Mysteries of Light)

The luminous mysteries, or mysteries of light, follow. This set of mysteries was added by Pope John Paul II in October 2002. The reason for the addition is that it completes the circle of Jesus's life, giving us a glimpse of the years between his baptism and his Passion. Those years are referred to as the years of Jesus's public ministry— when the person of Jesus is revealed as the Christ, the anointed one. This set, then, gives us the pictures of Jesus's life from his baptism in the Jordan River (see Matthew 3:16–17), the beginning of his public ministry, to his Transfiguration on a mountaintop with Peter, John, and James. The luminous mysteries focus on the light that Jesus brings into the world and into the hearts of people.

The Sorrowful Mysteries

The sorrowful mysteries reveal to us the suffering Jesus and Mary endured during his Passion and death. They begin with the agony in the garden, where Jesus prays with the desire and willingness to unite his own will to the will of God the Father, "Abba, Father, for you all things are possible; remove this cup from me; yet, not what I want, but what you want" (Mark 14:36). The set concludes with the Crucifixion and death of Jesus. The sorrowful mysteries give us a glimpse into the Passion of Jesus and of his mother, who shared in his suffering.

The Glorious Mysteries

Finally, the glorious mysteries tell us the story of Jesus's Resurrection through to the crowning of Mary as queen of heaven. As we know, the story does not end with Jesus on the cross or in the tomb; the story ends with a life renewed—Resurrection! These mysteries reveal to us Jesus's glory, a glory we will all share in one day, yet one in which Mary already shares, as seen in the last two mysteries of this set: her Assumption into heaven and her crowning as queen of heaven.

The glorious mysteries reveal the glory of the Resurrection and of life everlasting through both Jesus and Mary, which has been won for all humankind through Jesus Christ, our Lord.

Praying the Rosary

Praying the rosary is like sitting on the living room couch with Mary and opening up the family album. There is no one way to pray the rosary. We can pray it literally (simply praying the beads), meditatively (reflecting on the mysteries and the word of God in the Scriptures attributed to each mystery), or contemplatively (being, or resting, in the presence of God). Although many of us may begin with literal prayer, still burdened by the busyness of our daily routine, the rosary's aim is to lead us to contemplative prayer—into profound union with God. Just as the family album is a tool for remembering, so is the rosary—to both remember (walk through the memories) and re-member (come together).

By praying the rosary, we are led by Mary through the memories of her son's life, seeing the times they experienced great joy, growth, and promise; sorrow and suffering; and triumphant glory, thus invit-ing those moments into the present moment. Jesus's life compares to our own, and the chanting rhythm of Hail Marys invites us to connect the rhythm of our own lives—all that we experience in the here and now—to that of Jesus, where we experience a oneness, a heartbeat of unconditional love rooted in the bond of a relationship like no other.

Let Us Pray . . .

Begin with the Short, Dangling Strand of Beads

The rosary beads become a tool for us to get into the heart of Christ through Mary. The beginning short strand is anchored by the crucifix, to which all life points—a symbol of the suffering and death we endure in the circle of life leading to the joy of resurrection, which we are prom-ised through Christ. The prayer steps are as follows:

• **The Sign of the Cross.** Begin by holding the cross of the rosary in your right hand and making the sign of the cross.

- **The Apostles' Creed.** Profess the Apostles' Creed while holding the cross.

- **The Lord's Prayer.** Proceed to the first larger bead and pray the Lord's Prayer.

- **Three Hail Marys.** Pray the Hail Mary on the following three smaller beads.

- **The Doxology.** Conclude with the Doxology on the last larger bead of the short strand.

The Decades

As you begin the decades, you can use the following guidelines:

- **Announce the mystery.** Announce the type of mystery you would like to pray (you may choose to refer to the outline of the mysteries and the days attributed to praying them, on page 20). Announcing the mystery aloud calls us to focus on it and to enter the scene.

- **Listen to God's word and reflect on the mystery.** Consider the mystery. You can do this in a variety of ways: reading its scriptural context and meditating on it, meditating on the scriptural context and placing yourself at the scene, or contemplating the image of the face of Christ in an icon or a picture. When praying the rosary alone, as opposed to with a group, the possibilities for reflection are endless, allowing as much time and creativity as you would like to bring to your prayer. Open your heart and listen to God's word for you.

- **Enter the silence.** Take some time now to welcome the silence and to consider the story and what Jesus might be trying to say to you in this moment between friends when the hidden power of understanding exists.

- **Pray the decade.** After reflection, begin with the Lord's Prayer on the larger bead of the circlet, and then proceed through the ten smaller beads that follow by praying the Hail Mary on each of them. When you reach the next large bead, pray the Doxology. Take time to meditate on the next mystery, and conclude the silence with the Lord's Prayer. Proceed through the entire rosary until you have completed all decades.

Concluding Your Prayer of the Rosary

You can conclude praying the rosary in a variety of ways. Among the more common traditions are saying a prayer for the Holy Father and the whole Church. It is customary to conclude the rosary by praying for the intentions of our Holy Father. This is done in a variety of ways: some choose to simply offer the intentions of the Pope in praying the Hail Holy Queen; some by praying the Lord's Prayer, a Hail Mary, and the Doxology; while others choose to pray the small strand of beads again. By praying for the intentions of the Pope, we join in praying for the intentions and needs of the whole Church.

Hail Holy Queen *(Salve Regina)*
When the five decades are completed with a final prayer of the Doxology, pray the Hail Holy Queen. This prayer is one that honors Mary as queen of heaven and loving mother of us all—a mother who comes to our aid whenever we call on her and who shows to us her son, Jesus, in a more real and intimate way. In conjunction with its use at the end the rosary, it is often sung in its Latin form.

The Sign of the Cross
The rosary is completed just as it begins, with a final sign of the cross. *Note:* Many communities have added various prayers at the end of each decade or at the conclusion of the rosary. Those prayers are optional and should be directed to living the Christian life from the experience and fruits of praying the rosary, as outlined in the apostolic letter on the rosary, *Rosarium Virginis Mariae (RVM)*, written by Pope John Paul II in 2002.

Praying the Rosary Daily

The rosary can be prayed at many different times. Some prefer to pray it alone, while others like to join in with the community to pray it. Some will pray it before Mass, others during Eucharistic adoration. Let's remember that the rosary is given to us by God as an instrument to become unified with Christ, and therefore one another as God's Church.

The four sets of mysteries—the joyful, luminous, sorrowful, and glorious—are designated to be prayed on certain days of the week.

Taking into consideration particular feast days; the liturgical seasons followed by the Church—Advent, Christmas, Ordinary Time, Lent, and Easter; and what may be pastorally appropriate within a community (in other words, in times of war or suffering, joy or celebration); God also acknowledges the freedom in choosing the mysteries that will help the faithful to pray.

Day of the week	Set of mysteries to pray
Sunday	glorious mysteries
Monday	joyful mysteries
Tuesday	sorrowful mysteries
Wednesday	glorious mysteries
Thursday	luminous mysteries
Friday	sorrowful mysteries
Saturday	joyful mysteries

The benefit to designating a day of the week to the different mysteries is that it aids in unifying the Church in the rhythm of life, and for the Christian, it is a life of prayer. We begin on Sunday, the day of the Resurrection, and the rosary leads us through the life of Christ as we journey through the week. That pattern helps us to remain connected to Christ daily.

Praying three sets of mysteries, or twenty decades, is considered as having prayed a complete rosary. Praying twenty decades encompasses the life of Christ. Taking into consideration that many people are not able to pray the complete rosary (twenty decades) every day, the daily pattern outlined above allows for important contemplation on the life of Christ in the life of a disciple, young or old.

The Prayers of the Rosary

The Sign of the Cross

In the name of the Father, and of the Son, and of the Holy Spirit. Amen.

The Apostles' Creed

I believe in God, the Father almighty,
 creator of heaven and earth.
I believe in Jesus Christ, his only Son, our Lord.
 He was conceived by the power of the Holy Spirit
  and born of the Virgin Mary.
 He suffered under Pontius Pilate,
  was crucified, died, and was buried.
 He descended to the dead.
 On the third day he rose again.
 He ascended into heaven,
  and is seated at the right hand of the Father.
 He will come again to judge the living and the dead.

I believe in the Holy Spirit,
 the holy catholic Church,
 the communion of saints,
 the forgiveness of sins,
 the resurrection of the body,
 and the life everlasting.
 Amen.

The Lord's Prayer

Our Father, who art in heaven,
hallowed be thy name;
thy kingdom come;
thy will be done on earth as it is in heaven.
Give us this day our daily bread;
and forgive us our trespasses
as we forgive those who trespass against us;
and lead us not into temptation,
but deliver us from evil.
Amen.

The Hail Mary

Hail Mary, full of grace,
the Lord is with you!
Blessed are you among women,
and blessed is the fruit of your womb, Jesus.
Holy Mary, Mother of God,
pray for us sinners
now and at the hour of our death.
Amen.

The Doxology

Glory to the Father, and to the Son, and to the Holy Spirit:
as it was in the beginning, is now, and will be for ever.
Amen.

Hail Holy Queen *(Salve Regina)*

Hail, holy Queen, mother of Mercy,
hail, our life, our sweetness, and our hope.
To you we cry, the children of Eve;
to you we send up our sighs,
mourning and weeping in this land of exile.
Turn, then, most gracious advocate,
your eyes of mercy toward us;
lead us home at last
and show us the blessed fruit of your womb, Jesus:
O clement, O loving, O sweet Virgin Mary.

Closing Prayer (optional)

O God, whose only begotten Son, by his life, death, and Resurrection, has purchased for us the rewards of eternal life, grant, we beseech you, that meditating upon these mysteries of the most holy rosary of the Blessed Virgin Mary, we may imitate what they contain and obtain what they promise. Through the same Christ, our Lord. Amen. (Anne Vail, *Joy of the Rosary*, page 40)

Why Do We Pray the Rosary?

The rosary is one of the Church's most devotional prayers, a favorite of many Catholics who remain faithful to this simple yet profound rhythm of prayer. From the saints who have gone before us to the people who fill the pews on any given Sunday, the rosary remains a popular choice for prayer. But why? What is it about this continuous chant of Hail Marys that invites its use? Why has it remained one of the best-loved prayers of the Church, and why would a modern-day teenager want to pray it? What relevance does it have to the life of a young person of this third millennium?

To Feel the Rhythm of Human Life

Over the centuries countless Christians have turned to praying the rosary. And their reasons for praying it are as varied as the individuals themselves. Pope John Paul II, in his 2002 apostolic letter on the rosary, *Rosarium Virginis Mariae*, outlines many of the reasons why it is prayed so faithfully and why it has been so important to him:

> I myself have often encouraged the frequent recitation of the Rosary. From my youthful years this prayer has held an important place in my spiritual life. [. . .]. The Rosary has accompanied me in moments of joy and in moments of difficulty. To it I have entrusted any number of concerns; in it I have always found comfort. Twenty-four years ago, on 29 October 1978, scarcely two weeks after my election to the See of Peter, I frankly admitted: "The Rosary is my favourite prayer. A marvelous prayer! Marvelous in its simplicity and its depth. [. . .]. Against the background of the words *Ave Maria* the principal events of the life of Jesus Christ pass before the eyes of the soul. They take shape in the complete series of the joyful, sorrowful, and glorious mysteries, and they put us in living communion with Jesus through—we might say—the heart of his Mother. At the same time our heart can embrace in the decades of the Rosary all the events that make up the lives of individuals, families, nations, the Church, and all mankind. Our personal concerns and those of our

neighbor, especially those who are closest to us, who are dearest to us. Thus the simple prayer of the Rosary marks the rhythm of human life.[1]" (Number 2)

I set *the first year of my Pontificate* within the daily rhythm of the Rosary. Today, *as I begin the twenty-fifth year of my service as the Successor of Peter*, I wish to do the same. How many graces have I received in these years from the Blessed Virgin through the Rosary: *Magnificat anima mea Dominum!* I wish to lift up my thanks to the Lord in the words of his Most Holy Mother, under whose protection I have placed my Petrine ministry: *Totus Tuus!* (Number 2)

For Abundant Grace

Prayer is a two-way street. Sometimes we forget that God has a responsive part and that our prayer is never a monologue, but rather a dialogue. Every time we reach out to God in prayer, we always get a response. It can be frustrating at times because we may struggle to "hear" that response, or we may wonder if silence is all that we'll be left with. We may also struggle if God grants us something other than what we've prayed for or if the answer is delayed and not the immediate response we're wanting. Nonetheless, whenever we place ourselves before God in prayer, we can be sure of two things: God hears us and we receive God's grace. The real mystery about grace is that we don't have to do a thing to receive it. It is a gift from God that is constantly given to us. Grace is God "communicating to us at every moment of our existence" (*The Catholic Faith Handbook for Youth, [CFH], page 300). But in order to know that, it is really up to us to focus and become aware.

When was the last time you paid attention to your breathing? For those of us who suffer from asthma, allergies, or head colds, and for those who run, work out, or practice stress-relieving methods, attention to breathing becomes a priority. God's grace is like the air we breathe. It's always there, but how often do we really pay attention to it? Many times we don't until we really need to. Actually, without it, we die. It is the same in life—without God's grace, we die. How often do we really pay attention to *that?* Again, many times we don't until we really need to—during a breakup, the death of a friend or family member, the struggle through any number of various and very human situations. Thus, in our prayer and in our daily routine, it is important to listen, pay attention, and become aware of how God is present to us and responding, simply because we need God like the air we breathe. The rosary helps us to be more attentive to God's activity in our lives.

To Encounter Jesus, the Christ

The beauty of the mysteries is that they are inviting. The stories themselves welcome the disciple (that's you and me) to journey along. By meditating on the mysteries, we can enter the stories of the Gospels to encounter Jesus and to make the experience not only one of the past but also one of the present moment. Saint Ignatius himself used this form of prayer and made it popular.

By meditating on the mysteries, we come to know Jesus more intimately, in the same way his own mother knows and understands him, for it is Mary who leads us to him through the rosary. Our Holy Father reminds us that "it is not just a question of learning what he taught but of *'learning him.'* In this regard could we have any better teacher than Mary?" (*RVM,* number 14).

Any mother has an unbreakable bond with and an understanding of her child like no other, so it makes sense for us to approach Mary to come to know Jesus as she does. In our attempt to know him more intimately, not only do we share a friendship with him, but we naturally enter into his life and share his deepest feelings. Blessed Bartolo Longo suggests in his own writing on the rosary that the effect is the same "as two friends [who] frequently [spend time together][2]" (*RVM,* number 15). We all have the friend who can finish our sentences, the friend who can read our mind without words being said, the friend whom we imitate through quirky mannerisms and sayings. It seems that in spending more time together, we not only come to know each other quite well, we also start to act alike. And that precisely is our intent for praying—to encounter the holy so as to grow in holiness and love; to adopt the way of life of a model Christian, like Mary and the saints; and to grow more and more into the likeness of Jesus.

My first experience with the rosary was when I was just a child, attending Mass with my family. My mother's aunt was visiting, and I was sitting next to her in the pew. She was reciting the rosary after Communion and the organist was playing "Immaculate Mary." My great aunt was singing along in a low voice, "Ave, Ave, Ave Maria; Ave, Ave, Ave Maria." I was about eight or nine years old, and I welled up with tears, moved by her faith, by the beauty of the moment, and by the love I felt in my heart from the Mother of God.

Another occasion that sticks out in my mind was when I was in my twenties and on a pilgrimage to Medjugorje, a small town in Yugoslavia. We were in the parish church, hundreds of us crowded in, people from many countries praying in many different languages. As we prayed the first decade of the rosary, I could feel love spread through the room. When the decade was completed, the crowd, as one, began to sing in many different languages, "Ave, Ave, Ave Maria; Ave, Ave, Ave Maria." This time I sobbed. It felt like I was draining every sin, every negative conception I ever had of myself and all the negative things that people had said about me, and I was being filled with a vision of myself that God has—me as a special, beautiful person, loved completely, able to hold my head high and be anyone I wanted to be. I wept for all the things I had done to try to find out who I was, when in reality, I finally recognized who I was in God's eyes in that one special moment. I will never forget it. (John P. Campbell, 44, Madison, Connecticut)

For Unity with Our Christian Family

Through the act of praying the same prayer and through our connection with the communion of saints, we grow together in unity with our Christian family. The communion of saints is another way of describing the Church—all those who have faith in Jesus Christ. However, there are two factors to understand: "the spiritual practices that represent and bring about the unity of believers, and the actual communion that ties together all believers, both living and dead" (*CFH*, page 130). The unity of believers has to do with how we live as God's people. It includes all the ways we serve others, forgive others, and show mercy to others, and the reception of the sacraments. These works bond us together as Jesus's disciples: his family. The communion that unites all believers is about the Holy Spirit who unifies us all—those of us who still live on earth, those who have died and are being prepared to enter heaven and receive the fullness of God (a state called purgatory), and those who already share in the promise of heaven, including the saints.

Traditionally the rosary has been a means of uniting and strengthening the family. We've all heard the stories of our older generations as they share their memories of praying the rosary as a family—some humorous, others that evoke common responses of a child or an adolescent, and yet some very powerful. The experiences themselves reflect the struggles, frustrations, joys, and prayerfulness of life, as they should. But we all know that as much as we may "hem and haw" about our family times, those times pull us together more intimately. And if sharing a meal or participating in a game night together can do that, just think what praying together could do!

The rosary, then, is just one of the many ways we can be united and reconciled as a family, as Christ's Church, whether we're in church, on a retreat, or in our own living room.

For Peace

During my childhood, Latin was spoken at Mass. Unable to understand what was being said, my young mind would wander and my eyes observed the latest styles in clothing and hairdos. Inevitably, an "old person" nearby would have a set of rosary beads dangling from their hands while they knelt in prayer. My mind would pause and my eyes would always transfix on the small beads and crucifix. I would feel a sense of peace.

During my teen years, I often visited my grandmother to escape the badgering I'd receive from parents who, obviously, knew nothing about what it was like to be me. "Bub" would be sitting on her front porch, making the neighborhood safe for everyone, while she prayed her rosary. I'd walk onto the porch, see her praying, and feel a sense of peace.

In my forties, my father was terminally ill. A feeling of help-lessness consumed me. There had to be something I could do to make him well. I prayed the rosary, found peace, and was able to help my dad go in peace. (Joan LaRochelle, 52, Chelmsford, Massachusetts)

In practice the rosary has become a popular prayer in times of war, bloodshed, and violence. Pope Leo XIII proposed that the rosary was "an effective spiritual weapon against the evils afflicting society" (*RVM*, number 2). What we come to realize is that we cannot pray the rosary only for God's action. We cannot pray this prayer without it having a profound effect on us. We cannot pray this prayer without becoming committed to taking a proactive part in working toward peace in our world, in our communities, in our schools, in our workplaces, in our homes, and in our hearts. If we want peace, we must turn to, learn from, and unify ourselves with Christ, the very source of peace. The rosary leads us there.

For Contemplation

My experience with the rosary began when I was a teen. I was a young and inexperienced girl, in the full scope of life and the world, and very shy. My feelings at the time were of fear—of not belonging or fitting in, of not being popular, smart enough, pretty enough, slim enough—all the typical things of self-esteem that filled my head with doubts. It was at this point that I found myself with rosary in hand and was taught how to pray and meditate on the life of Jesus. I slept with my rosary, I carried it with me, and I would say at least one decade a day, usually falling asleep. Did I have a profound experience? No. Did I have a life experience? Yes. Prayer of any form is a relational experience. I'm telling you this from the vantage point of a sixty-one-year-old woman. The rosary and Mary gave me security and a safety net when I was young. What I didn't realize then was that I was building a relationship with the family of God through Mary. She became my silent heart-mother and, true to her call in life, stayed by my side. Fears are gone, and in my heart I know Jesus, God the Father, and the Holy Spirit. Self-esteem fears are a thing of the past. The rosary ritual, for me, was the beginning of a life adventure leading me into the truth of who I am and who I am meant to be in this world and in the next. Enjoy your journey with all the gifts that are offered, because they lead you to a place of joy and safety. (Carolyn Della Pietra, 61, Hamden, Connecticut)

Contemplation is what Saint John of the Cross calls "silent love" (*CFH,* page 326). It is an intimate union with God, a true oneness. Many of the saints experienced contemplative prayer, as did many people throughout the centuries, including many today. Pope John Paul II wrote, "The Rosary belongs among the finest and most praiseworthy traditions of Christian contemplation" (*RVM,* number 5). That is simply because as one prays the rosary, one cannot help but contemplate the life of Christ. What is common to all experiences of contemplative prayer is a profound awareness of God's presence. It is an experience where words are not needed, but where there is understanding; where love is the only language needed and known. Contemplation is all about *being,* not *doing.*

The life of a disciple is a life of prayer. The rosary helps us as individuals and as Christian communities to live it.

To Experience Mary's Love

Three years ago my grandmother was diagnosed with kidney failure and needed a transplant. This news made everyone in my family extremely nervous and afraid. As it turned out, my mom was found to be a compatible match to my grandmother. My mom donated her kidney to her and was forever changed by it.

In an effort to protect my family, I built a wall around my emotions. Feeling scared and all alone, I finally opened my heart to God and asked for his help. Given the situation and knowing that I needed a mother's strength to draw on, God gave me Mary. I became increasingly aware of her presence in my life, and I found myself with an increased desire to form a closer bond with her. So I bought a book and taught myself how to pray the rosary. I began to pray a different set of mysteries each day and grew more and more devoted to Mary.

Because the mysteries of the rosary teach us the story of Jesus's life, death, and Resurrection, I began to develop a powerful relationship with Jesus. I found myself trying to model him in thought and action, and it was through praying the sorrowful mysteries that I was able to find the strength I needed to go through with the operation.

Through my praying the rosary, Mary led me to Jesus. (Robin Adams, 40, Chelmsford, Massachusetts)

Ever since, my mom has been a much more spiritual person, and she prays the rosary several times a week. My mom was the first person to teach me how to pray the rosary. She taught me what the rosary means to her and why she prays it. I have said the rosary with my mom a couple of times, and it now means something to me. For me the rosary is an easy way to connect with God on a strong level. The rosary is also a good way to honor Mary. The rosary has affected my mom in such a positive way, and it has helped her grow close to God. The rosary has the potential to affect everyone in the way that it has affected my mom. I hope that it can affect my life like it has affected my mom's. (Matthew Adams, 16, Chelmsford, Massachusetts)

There's *something* about Mary. Just as God is responsive to our prayer, so is Mary when we ask for her intercession (prayer on our behalf). The most perfect of mothers cannot help but reach out to us and plead for us. Through our praying the rosary, we engage Mary in the dialogue—she prays not only for us but with us. She places our needs at the feet of her son. Throughout the nineteenth and twentieth centuries, we have seen and heard Mary's response, recalling her apparitions at Lourdes and Fatima. There she pleaded with us to become a people of prayer, through the rosary, to unify ourselves to the will of God—just as she did with her own yes—and to become a people of peace.

Through the rosary we come to intimately know Mary as mother. Just as she watched over Jesus in his growing up, she now watches over us in the same way—loving, nurturing, and forming us, as she did Jesus. Because we are the mystical body of her son, Jesus, in the world, she becomes our mother, too.

At the close of his apostolic letter, the Pope reminds us that the rosary is "a spiritual aid which should not be underestimated" (*RVM*, number 42).

Getting Ready to Pray

We've read the stories of those whose lives have been affected by this prayer, their devotions to the Blessed Mother who has interceded for them with a perfect motherly love, and we've come to have a better understanding of this great gift of the Church, the rosary. I leave you with the empowering and concluding words of John Paul II in *Rosarium Virginis Mariae,* a special commissioning of young people: "I look to all of you, . . . and to you, young people: *confidently take up the Rosary once again.* Rediscover the Rosary in the light of Scripture, in harmony with the Liturgy, and in the context of your daily lives" (number 43).

> May the graces and blessings that flow from this ancient of prayers, prayed faithfully by so many in the present and of old, help you to grow in holiness and in intimacy with the God of love, a God who believes in you, trusts in you, and counts on you with his whole being, with his whole life. Holy Mary, Mother of God, pray for us, showing us the way to your son. Amen.

CHAPTER 2

The Joyful Mysteries

Begin the joyful mysteries with the following prayers:

◆ **The Sign of the Cross.** Hold the cross of the rosary in your right hand and make the sign of the cross: "In the name of the Father, and of the Son, and of the Holy Spirit. Amen."

◆ **The Apostles' Creed.** Profess the Apostles' Creed while you are holding the cross:

I believe in God, the Father almighty,
    creator of heaven and earth.
I believe in Jesus Christ, his only Son, our Lord.
        He was conceived by the power of the Holy Spirit
            and born of the Virgin Mary.
        He suffered under Pontius Pilate,
            was crucified, died, and was buried.
        He descended to the dead.
        On the third day he rose again.
        He ascended into heaven,
            and is seated at the right hand of the Father.
        He will come again to judge the living and the dead.
I believe in the Holy Spirit,
        the holy catholic Church,
        the communion of saints,
        the forgiveness of sins,
        the resurrection of the body,
        and the life everlasting.
        Amen.

- **The Lord's Prayer.** Proceed to the first larger bead and pray the Lord's Prayer:

> Our Father, who art in heaven,
> hallowed be thy name;
> thy kingdom come;
> thy will be done on earth as it is in heaven.
> Give us this day our daily bread;
> and forgive us our trespasses
> as we forgive those who trespass against us;
> and lead us not into temptation,
> but deliver us from evil.
> Amen.

- **Three Hail Marys.** Pray the Hail Mary on the following three smaller beads:

> Hail Mary, full of grace,
> the Lord is with you!
> Blessed are you among women,
> and blessed is the fruit of your womb, Jesus.
> Holy Mary, Mother of God,
> pray for us sinners
> now and at the hour of our death.
> Amen.

- **The Doxology.** Conclude with the Doxology on the last larger bead of the short strand:

> Glory to the Father, and to the Son, and to the Holy Spirit:
> as it was in the beginning, is now, and will be for ever.
> Amen.

The First Joyful Mystery: The Annunciation

Listen to God's Word

> In the sixth month the angel Gabriel was sent by God to a town in Galilee called Nazareth, to a virgin engaged to a man whose name was Joseph, of the house of David. The virgin's name was

Mary. And he came to her and said, "Greetings, favored one! The Lord is with you." But she was much perplexed by his words and pondered what sort of greeting this might be. The angel said to her, "Do not be afraid, Mary, for you have found favor with God. And now, you will conceive in your womb and bear a son, and you will name him Jesus. He will be great, and will be called the Son of the Most High, and the Lord God will give to him the throne of his ancestor David. He will reign over the house of Jacob forever, and of his kingdom there will be no end." Mary said to the angel, "How can this be, since I am a virgin?" The angel said to her, "The Holy Spirit will come upon you, and the power of the Most High will overshadow you; therefore the child to be born will be holy; he will be called Son of God. And now, your relative Elizabeth in her old age has also conceived a son; and this is the sixth month for her who was said to be barren. For nothing will be impossible with God." Then Mary said, "Here am I, the servant of the Lord; let it be with me according to your word." Then the angel departed from her. (Luke 1:26–38)

Reflect on the Mystery

Two summers ago I attended World Youth Day in Toronto. It was the day before our trek to the field for Mass with the Pope. That day the Boston Archdiocese was having Mass together with the cardinal. After Communion the cardinal asked those who would consider the priesthood or leading a religious life to come up to the altar for a special blessing. I had no idea what to do. Like most sixteen-year-olds, I was uncertain about my future, and I didn't want to rule out anything. The one thing I did know about my future, though, was that I didn't want my relationship with God to change at all. I was happy with our relationship. I was involved in youth ministry and felt spiritually alive. A lot of adults had told me that in their young-adult and college years, they felt disconnected from God; their relationship had weakened. That's not what I wanted. I didn't want to leave high school and the structured faith that helped me strengthen my relationship with God. I was pretty certain that going to church every Sunday would be a little harder when I didn't have my parents dragging me out of bed. Was becoming a nun the answer? It would definitely give me the structure I relied on so heavily. I decided to go up to the altar, believing that a blessing never hurt anyone. There were about twenty of us, both girls and boys, who made our way to the altar. And there I had the most moving experience of my life. The cardinal raised his hand over us for the blessing, and I just started crying and crying and crying. I couldn't stop, and I didn't even know why I started. I was totally filled with emotion, more than I ever have been in my entire life. When I looked around, other people were crying, too. The weirdest part was that I wasn't sad. I was not crying because I was hurt or upset. I was simply (if anything like this is simple) filled from head to toe with the Holy Spirit. When I returned to my seat, I was relieved; I could breathe again. I realized as I sat down that I don't need to become a nun to keep God in my life because he's always going to be with me, whether I know it or not; whether I want him to be or not. But it's up to me to keep that line of communication and love open. We have to choose if we want Christ in our lives or not, and we don't necessarily have to become priests or nuns or deacons to keep him there. God calls people to many vocations. In Baptism we became committed to God; he is part of us. I have chosen to have Christ in my life and to follow him because it gives me a sense of belonging and security, and because he loves me unconditionally. I know that his Holy Spirit will always be there to lift me up when I have fallen into doubt or despair. (Kathleen Massey, 17, Chelmsford, Massachusetts)

Enter the Silence

Take some time to reflect in silence on God's word and how it is speaking to you in this moment.

Intention for Prayer (optional)

Lord, I pray that I may respond to your call for me even when I am given a difficult decision to make that will require total giving of myself. Help me to not be afraid and to always trust you. Amen.

Pray the Decade

- ◆ Our Father . . .

- ◆ Hail Mary . . . *[Using the next ten beads, repeat ten in succession.]*

- ◆ Glory to . . .

The Second Joyful Mystery: The Visitation

Listen to God's Word

In those days Mary set out and went with haste to a Judean town in the hill country, where she entered the house of Zechariah and greeted Elizabeth. When Elizabeth heard Mary's greeting, the child leaped in her womb. And Elizabeth was filled with the Holy Spirit and exclaimed with a loud cry, "Blessed are you among women, and blessed is the fruit of your womb. And why has this happened to me, that the mother of my Lord comes to me? For as soon as I heard the sound of your greeting, the child in my womb leaped for joy. And blessed is she who believed that there would be a fulfillment of what was spoken to her by the Lord."

And Mary said,

"My soul magnifies the Lord,
    and my spirit rejoices in God my
        Savior,
for he has looked with favor on the
        lowliness of his servant.
    Surely, from now on all generations
        will call me blessed;

for the Mighty One has done great things
   for me,
     and holy is his name.
His mercy is for those who fear him
     from generation to generation.
He has shown strength with his arm;
     he has scattered the proud in the thoughts of their
        hearts.
He has brought down the powerful from their thrones,
     and lifted up the lowly;
he has filled the hungry with good things,
     and sent the rich away empty.
He has helped his servant Israel,
     in remembrance of his mercy,
according to the promise he made to our ancestors,
     to Abraham and to his descendants forever."
   And Mary remained with her about three months and
     then returned to her home.

(Luke 1:39–56)

Reflect on the Mystery

My uncle is in the army and was serving in Iraq this past Christmas (2003). As part of his Christmas package, we all had our pictures taken and wrote messages to him on them. Feeling inspired by the Holy Spirit, I wrote a prayer that just flowed from my heart.

As Christmas drew closer, I decided I would tell the story about my uncle and write a similar prayer for the people on my e-mail list. I never knew the impact my message would make!

I got amazing responses from my e-mail—all positive and encouraging, but one stood out. It was from my e-mail pal in Chicago. She wrote telling me how my e-mail had put her in the Christmas spirit she had been missing. She wrote about how she realized what her family meant to her. Then she continued, saying that even though she wasn't a Christian, she felt inspired to pray for the first time ever. She prayed for her family as well as mine! Right then, as I read her e-mail with tear-filled eyes, I realized that God had used me in an amazing way to share his glory! (Liza D., 16, Milton, Vermont)

Enter the Silence

Take some time to reflect in silence on God's word and how it is speaking to you in this moment.

Intention for Prayer (optional)

Lord, bless the people in my life with whom I am able to share faith and who help me to encounter you more intimately. Amen.

Pray the Decade

+ Our Father . . .

+ Hail Mary . . . *[Repeat ten in succession.]*

+ Glory to . . .

The Third Joyful Mystery: The Birth of Our Lord

Listen to God's Word

> In those days a decree went out from Emperor Augustus that all the world should be registered. This was the first registration and was taken while Quirinius was governor of Syria. All went to their own towns to be registered. Joseph also went from the town of Nazareth in Galilee to Judea, to the city of David called Bethlehem, because he was descended from the house and family of David. He went to be registered with Mary, to whom he was engaged and who was expecting a child. While they were there, the time came for her to deliver her child. And she gave birth to her firstborn son

and wrapped him in bands of cloth, and laid him in a manger, because there was no place for them in the inn.

In that region there were shepherds living in the fields, keeping watch over their flock by night. Then an angel of the Lord stood before them, and the glory of the Lord shone around them, and they were terrified. But the angel said to them, "Do not be afraid; for see—I am bringing you good news of great joy for all the people: to you is born this day in the city of David a Savior, who is the Messiah, the Lord. This will be a sign for you: you will find a child wrapped in bands of cloth and lying in a manger." And suddenly there was with the angel a multitude of the heavenly host, praising God and saying,

"Glory to God in the highest heaven,
and on earth peace among those whom he favors!"

When the angels had left them and gone into heaven, the shepherds said to one another, "Let us go now to Bethlehem and see this thing that has taken place, which the Lord has made known to us." So they went with haste and found Mary and Joseph, and the child lying in the manger. When they saw this, they made known what had been told them about this child; and all who heard it were amazed at what the shepherds told them. But Mary treasured all these words and pondered them in her heart. The shepherds returned, glorifying and praising God for all they had heard and seen, as it had been told them. (Luke 2:1–20)

Reflect on the Mystery

In the fall of 1999, I went to Jamaica and discovered Jesus. My mother and I traveled in a group with Food for the Poor to witness the suffering of the destitute. We were in one building that housed disabled and mentally handicapped children. As our group reached out to the children, I followed my mom around for a while. I wanted to help, but I was too shy. I found myself just standing there, spiritually walled-in and totally isolated. I walked over to my mom and shared with her how I was feeling. She said that I simply had to let go and give of myself. I took a deep breath and found myself next to a little girl alone in a wheelchair. She could not see because she was blind,

but she reached out her beautiful chocolate-brown hand and I grasped it. I found myself gently stroking her cheek while she firmly held on to my wrist. As a grateful tear escaped my misty eyes, I realized that I was encountering Jesus face to face in the disguise of the poor, but I had to give totally of myself to reach out and find him. (Cristina Marie Garcia del Busto, 18, Orlando, Florida)

Enter the Silence

Take some time to reflect in silence on God's word and how it is speaking to you in this moment.

Intention for Prayer (optional)

Lord, I pray that whenever you reveal yourself to me, or when you present me with goodness, I may be changed into becoming more like you, simply by the encounter. Amen.

Pray the Decade

+ Our Father . . .
+ Hail Mary . . . *[Repeat ten in succession.]*
+ Glory to . . .

The Fourth Joyful Mystery: The Presentation of Jesus in the Temple

Listen to God's Word

> When the time came for their purification according to the law of Moses, they brought him up to Jerusalem to present him to the Lord

(as it is written in the law of the Lord, "Every firstborn male shall be designated as holy to the Lord"), and they offered a sacrifice according to what is stated in the law of the Lord, "a pair of turtledoves or two young pigeons."

Now there was a man in Jerusalem whose name was Simeon; this man was righteous and devout, looking forward to the consolation of Israel, and the Holy Spirit rested on him. It had been revealed to him by the Holy Spirit that he would not see death before he had seen the Lord's Messiah. Guided by the Spirit, Simeon came into the temple; and when the parents brought in the child Jesus, to do for him what was customary under the law, Simeon took him in his arms and praised God, saying,

"Master, now you are dismissing your servant in peace,
    according to your word;
for my eyes have seen your salvation,
    which you have prepared in the presence of all peoples,
a light for revelation to the Gentiles
    and for glory to your people Israel."

And the child's father and mother were amazed at what was being said about him. Then Simeon blessed them and said to his mother Mary, "This child is destined for the falling and the rising of many in Israel, and to be a sign that will be opposed so that the inner thoughts of many will be revealed—and a sword will pierce your own soul too."

There was also a prophet, Anna the daughter of Phanuel, of the tribe of Asher. She was of a great age, having lived with her husband seven years after her marriage, then as a widow to the age of eighty-four. She never left the temple but worshiped there with fasting and prayer night and day. At that moment she came, and began to praise God and to speak about the child to all who were looking for the redemption of Jerusalem. (Luke 2:22–38)

Reflect on the Mystery

At work camp 2003, I went in with an open mind to help people in need. At the end of the week, I felt that I had served God and his community well. I knew that by serving God I would feel good within myself and that that would be my "thank you" from him—but he did a little more for me.

My best friend, Brian, was with me at work camp that year, and we were baby-sitting little kids as a community project. While baby-sitting these kids, I saw a twinkle in Brian's eyes, like God had reached out and touched him through the kids. As Brian dazed off, staring at this little boy that looked up to him with the biggest, glazed, young eyes, he realized that even the littlest things can make you see God working in all his ways.

At the end of the week, Brian pulled me aside and tearfully told me that he felt a stronger connection with God and that I helped him along the way. During that week I was shown that God can reach the hardest people and touch their hearts. Since that one week at work camp, God has opened a door between my friend and me and has made our friendship become the best friendship ever. (Amanda Konrad, 16, Mason, Ohio)

Enter the Silence

Take some time to reflect in silence on God's word and how it is speaking to you in this moment.

Intention for Prayer (optional)

Lord, give me the eyes of faith to see you so that I may recognize you in the people I meet and through the gifts that come from you—so that I may become aware of what is holy in my life. Amen.

Pray the Decade

◆ Our Father . . .

◆ Hail Mary . . . *[Repeat ten in succession.]*

◆ Glory to . . .

The Fifth Joyful Mystery:
The Finding of Jesus in the Temple

Listen to God's Word

Now every year his parents went to Jerusalem for the festival of the Passover. And when he was twelve years old, they went up as usual for the festival. When the festival was ended and they started to return, the boy Jesus stayed behind in Jerusalem, but his parents did not know it. Assuming that he was in the group of travelers, they went a day's journey. Then they started to look for him among their relatives and friends. When they did not find him, they returned to Jerusalem to search for him. After three days they found him in the temple, sitting among the teachers, listening to them and asking them questions. And all who heard him were amazed at his understanding and his answers. When his parents saw him they were astonished; and his mother said to him, "Child, why have you treated us like this? Look, your father and I have been searching for you in great anxiety." He said to them, "Why were you searching for me? Did you not know that I must be in my Father's house?" But they did not understand what he said to them. Then he went down with them and came to Nazareth, and was obedient to them. His mother treasured all these things in her heart.

And Jesus increased in wisdom and in years, and in divine and human favor. (Luke 2:41–52)

Reflect on the Mystery

Life is a combination of many great and small events that shape the persons we are becoming. In my life, one event that forever changed me was attending high school. You're probably thinking, "Everyone goes to high school, what's the big deal?" I made the decision in the eighth grade to attend an all-girls' Catholic high school instead of the public school my friends would be attending. I struggled my freshman year, being away from my friends and going to a new school. My friends didn't understand the decision I was making because they couldn't understand why I would want to leave them and go to a school where none of my friends would be. All my friends had been in

public schools for their entire lives, and there wasn't a question of where they would go to high school. They were shocked and disappointed when I told them of my decision—something I thought was good news. Despite their disappointment, somehow I knew I was making the right decision.

Sometime between that first day of ninth grade and now, only weeks from graduation, I realized that I've changed. Because of my high school decision, I am now a more confident person. I was elected student government president my junior year. If you had told me three years ago that I would be holding such an office, I would have told you that you were crazy. It is because of the people in my life and the lessons I have learned in high school that I have become a more self-assured person.

I think God has helped me become the person I am today. He was there through everything— guiding my decisions and always looking out for me. (Emily Ryan, 18, Cincinnati, Ohio)

Enter the Silence

Take some time to reflect in silence on God's word and how it is speaking to you in this moment.

Intention for Prayer (optional)

Lord, I pray that I may not be afraid to respond to your call for me, even when I, or others, might not understand. Amen.

Pray the Decade

♦ Our Father . . .

♦ Hail Mary . . . *[Repeat ten in succession.]*

♦ Glory to . . .

Concluding the Joyful Mysteries

To conclude the joyful mysteries, say the following prayers:

◆ **The Doxology**

> Glory to the Father, and to the Son, and to the Holy Spirit:
> as it was in the beginning, is now, and will be for ever.
> Amen.

◆ **Hail Holy Queen** *(Salve Regina)*

> Hail, holy Queen, mother of Mercy,
> hail, our life, our sweetness, and our hope.
> To you we cry, the children of Eve;
> to you we send up our sighs,
> mourning and weeping in this land of exile.
> Turn, then, most gracious advocate,
> your eyes of mercy toward us;
> lead us home at last
> and show us the blessed fruit of your womb, Jesus:
> O clement, O loving, O sweet Virgin Mary.

You may end here or continue with these words:

> Pray for us, O holy Mother of God, that we may be made worthy
> of the promises of Christ. Let us pray.

◆ **Closing Prayer** (optional)

> O God, whose only begotten Son, by his life, death, and Resur-
> rection, has purchased for us the rewards of eternal life, grant, we
> beseech you, that meditating upon these mysteries of the most
> holy rosary of the Blessed Virgin Mary, we may imitate what they
> contain and obtain what they promise. Through the same Christ,
> our Lord. Amen. (Anne Vail, *Joy of the Rosary*, page 40)

◆ **The Sign of the Cross.** "In the name of the Father, and of the Son,
and of the Holy Spirit. Amen."

CHAPTER 3

The Luminous Mysteries (The Mysteries of Light)

Begin the luminous mysteries with the following prayers:

+ **The Sign of the Cross.** Hold the cross of the rosary in your right hand and make the sign of the cross: "In the name of the Father, and of the Son, and of the Holy Spirit. Amen."

+ **The Apostles' Creed.** Profess the Apostles' Creed while you are holding the cross:

> I believe in God, the Father almighty,
>   creator of heaven and earth.
> I believe in Jesus Christ, his only Son, our Lord.
>   He was conceived by the power of the Holy Spirit
>   and born of the Virgin Mary.
>   He suffered under Pontius Pilate,
>   was crucified, died, and was buried.
>   He descended to the dead.
>   On the third day he rose again.
>   He ascended into heaven,
>   and is seated at the right hand of the Father.
>   He will come again to judge the living and the dead.
>
> I believe in the Holy Spirit,
>   the holy catholic Church,
>   the communion of saints,
>   the forgiveness of sins,
>   the resurrection of the body,
>   and the life everlasting.
>   Amen.

- **The Lord's Prayer.** Proceed to the first larger bead and pray the Lord's Prayer:

> Our Father, who art in heaven,
> hallowed be thy name;
> thy kingdom come;
> thy will be done on earth as it is in heaven.
> Give us this day our daily bread;
> and forgive us our trespasses
> as we forgive those who trespass against us;
> and lead us not into temptation,
> but deliver us from evil.
> Amen.

- **Three Hail Marys.** Pray the Hail Mary on the following three smaller beads:

> Hail Mary, full of grace,
> the Lord is with you!
> Blessed are you among women,
> and blessed is the fruit of your womb, Jesus.
> Holy Mary, Mother of God,
> pray for us sinners
> now and at the hour of our death.
> Amen.

- **The Doxology.** Conclude with the Doxology on the last larger bead of the short strand:

> Glory to the Father, and to the Son, and to the Holy Spirit:
> as it was in the beginning, is now, and will be for ever.
> Amen.

The First Luminous Mystery: The Baptism of Jesus

Listen to God's Word

> Then Jesus came from Galilee to John at the Jordan, to be baptized by him. John would have prevented him, saying, "I need to be baptized by you, and do you come to me?" But Jesus answered

him, "Let it be so now; for it is proper for us in this way to fulfill all righteousness." Then he consented. And when Jesus had been baptized, just as he came up from the water, suddenly the heavens were opened to him and he saw the Spirit of God descending like a dove and alighting on him. And a voice from heaven said, "This is my Son, the Beloved, with whom I am well pleased." (Matthew 3:13–17)

Reflect on the Mystery

I've always known that God has a plan for everyone, but only through recent events have I come to realize that God is pleased with me and sees me as beloved. A few months ago, I found out that my school drama club was producing *Godspell* for its spring musical. I thought that being a part of the play would help me use my talents in the best way possible. Every night before the audition, I sincerely prayed, letting God know that making *Godspell* was not only the best way I could praise him but also something that I wanted more than anything. I was crushed when the cast list did not have my name on it. The chance I sought to glorify God with the talents he gave me was lost. However, a month later I auditioned for *Once Upon a Mattress* with a local company. Even though I made the musical, I still wanted *Godspell*. Now, being in *Once Upon a Mattress* has become an exciting, fulfilling, and rewarding time in my life. I am unique and special in God's eyes, and I believe that God always leads me to the right path; it is just up to me to choose it. He has a plan for me, and even if I don't foresee it, I still know that it is for the best. I have come to understand the words of Jesus's, "Let it be so now, for it is proper for us in this way to fulfill all righteousness" (Matthew 3:15). (Margaret Jumonville, 15, Baton Rouge, Louisiana)

Enter the Silence

Take some time to reflect in silence on God's word and how it is speaking to you in this moment.

Intention for Prayer (optional)

Lord, may I always have a sense of your love for me as your child—your "Beloved," with whom you are well pleased—just as I am. And when I feel defeated by my faults and failings, my sin, and my feelings of not being good enough, come and find me and light my way to the hope and love you have for me. Amen.

Pray the Decade

- ◆ Our Father . . .
- ◆ Hail, Mary . . . *[Using the next ten beads, repeat ten in succession.]*
- ◆ Glory be . . .

The Second Luminous Mystery: Jesus Reveals Himself in the Miracle at Cana

Listen to God's Word

On the third day there was a wedding in Cana of Galilee, and the mother of Jesus was there. Jesus and his disciples had also been invited to the wedding. When the wine gave out, the mother of Jesus said to him, "They have no wine." And Jesus said to her, "Woman, what concern is that to you and to me? My hour has not yet come." His mother said to the servants, "Do whatever he tells you." Now standing there were six stone water jars for the Jewish rites of purification, each holding twenty or thirty gallons. Jesus said to them, "Fill the jars with water." And they filled them

up to the brim. He said to them, "Now draw some out, and take it to the chief steward." So they took it. When the steward tasted the water that had become wine, and did not know where it came from (though the servants who had drawn the water knew), the steward called the bridegroom and said to him, "Everyone serves the good wine first, and then the inferior wine after the guests have become drunk. But you have kept the good wine until now." Jesus did this, the first of his signs, in Cana of Galilee, and re-vealed his glory; and his disciples believed in him.

After this he went down to Capernaum with his mother, his brothers, and his disciples; and they remained there a few days. (John 2:1–12)

Reflect on the Mystery

Many people described me as a follower and not a leader. I played the roles everyone wanted me to play. But, deep down in ourselves, we have hidden talents and gifts that we find through the help of someone else.

The summer of my sophomore year, my sister requested I go to a summer leadership camp. I didn't want to go to camp! I questioned if I would make friends. My sister proved me wrong, because I met many new friends there. I approached people, something I would never do before. One session included a reflection on love. We were reminded that someone loved us and believed in us. At the end of the reflection, I gave my sister a big hug and told her how much I loved her, and how much her support meant to me. She believed in me as a leader and not a follower; she saw something in me that I did not see.

Since I went to camp, I am open to new things. I find goodness in myself and all of life. I am now the president of our school's biggest community-service organization. My sister's belief in me is why I am a leader. Leadership is my gift from God. (Katie Barnett, 17, Cincinnati, Ohio)

Enter the Silence

Take some time to reflect in silence on God's word and how it is speaking to you in this moment.

Intention for Prayer (optional)

Lord, thank you for the people in my life who believe in me simply because they trust your Holy Spirit, who lives within me and works through me. Thank you for the times they recognize me as your child—your very own creation—anointed, called, and gifted. Amen.

Pray the Decade

* Our Father . . .

* Hail Mary . . . *[Repeat ten in succession.]*

* Glory to . . .

The Third Luminous Mystery: Jesus Proclaims the Good News of the Kingdom of God

Listen to God's Word

Now after John was arrested, Jesus came to Galilee, proclaiming the good news of God, and saying, "The time is fulfilled, and the kingdom of God has come near; repent, and believe in the good news." (Mark 1:14–15)

Reflect on the Mystery

I had been having a rough time trying to figure out who I actually was, but most of all, I had a hard time finding God. He wasn't truly a part of my life because I didn't invite him into my heart. I had gone on my first Tahoe retreat, and I didn't know anyone who was going except for a few people who were from my church. Throughout the week I had figured that this retreat was not working for me, until that Wednesday. We were told that we could receive the sacrament of Penance and Reconciliation. I didn't understand the whole process, or the point of it, and I asked my group leader what happens. She explained to me that you can go to a priest and confess your sins. I had figured that I had done some wrong things in my life, but none that I wanted to admit to. My leader told me that I should go—just for a blessing. I said, "Sure, why not?" When I got in line, I took in my surroundings. Everyone was crying. I couldn't understand, but then I found myself crying. As I got up to the priest, I ended up confessing everything to him. By the time I had finished, the sun was setting. I decided to go for a walk. I found a great cliff to sit on and watch the sun set. As I watched it, I felt a sense of relief in my soul. Everything I had done wrong in my life had gone away, and as the sun set, at the last second, I felt God's connection within me. It was warmth and love at the same time, something I hadn't fully experienced for a long time. I knew God was with me that day, and I keep going back to that same spot every year, just to feel the warmth again. (Ashton D. Cozzo, 17, San Jose, California)

Enter the Silence

Take some time to reflect in silence on God's word and how it is speaking to you in this moment.

Intention for Prayer (optional)

Lord, take my hands and feet, my voice and thoughts, and all the love I have to give, and make them yours. You call me "salt of the earth . . . light of the world" (Matthew 5:13–14). Bless me to be a builder of the Kingdom here on Earth: through my giving to poor people in other countries, standing up for what is right in my own country, being a responsible member of my community, treating everyone equally and with respect at my school, becoming involved in my parish, and loving and caring for my family—but to start by paying special attention to what is in my very own heart. Amen.

Pray the Decade

* Our Father . . .

* Hail Mary . . . *[Repeat ten in succession.]*

* Glory to . . .

The Fourth Luminous Mystery: The Transfiguration of Jesus

Listen to God's Word

> Now about eight days after these sayings Jesus took with him Peter and John and James, and went up on the mountain to pray. And while he was praying, the appearance of his face changed, and his clothes became dazzling white. Suddenly they saw two men, Moses and Elijah, talking to him. They appeared in glory and were speaking of his departure, which he was about to accomplish at Jerusalem. Now Peter and his companions were weighed down with sleep; but since they had stayed awake, they saw his glory and the two men who stood with him. Just as they were leaving him, Peter said to Jesus, "Master, it is good for us to be here; let us make three dwellings, one for you, one for Moses, and one for Elijah"—not knowing what he said. While he was saying this, a cloud came and overshadowed them; and they were terrified as they entered the cloud. Then from the cloud

came a voice that said, "This is my Son, my Chosen; listen to him!" When the voice had spoken, Jesus was found alone. And they kept silent and in those days told no one any of the things they had seen. (Luke 9:28–36)

Reflect on the Mystery

"Mom, am I going to die?" was the first question out of my mouth when I was diagnosed with diabetes. I was unable to comprehend the pain and sympathy my family was feeling for me. Inside I was feeling empty and alone, knowing that I was never going to be normal again.

Nothing seemed the same anymore. Everyone who was my friend seemed like my enemy, as they could eat chocolate while I got a needle shoved in my stomach. I felt like I was alone in my own little bubble trying to reach out to the world, but no one was hearing me. They were deaf to my situation. I didn't know how to explain the collision of thoughts in my head: "Why me?" or "Why is God punishing me?" I was just stuck on a cliff waiting to figure out which way to go.

In the end I figured out the answer to those questions, and "Why me?" turned into "I am so lucky." Having diabetes has made me a more responsible person, and that has made my dreams become a reality. I consider my disease to be a gift from God because it gives me a challenge that I can try to overcome every day of my life. Today I look back on my life and I can't see where I would be without the challenges brought about from my diabetes, and someday I hope to find a cure for the millions of people who live with the disease. (Justine Noel Coyne, 17, Simi Valley, California)

Enter the Silence

Take some time to reflect in silence on God's word and how it is speaking to you in this moment.

Intention for Prayer (optional)

Lord, change me so that I may reflect your glory by the life I live right now. Amen.

Pray the Decade

+ Our Father . . .
+ Hail Mary . . . *[Repeat ten in succession.]*
+ Glory to . . .

The Fifth Luminous Mystery: The Institution of the Eucharist

Listen to God's Word

On the first day of Unleavened Bread, when the Passover lamb is sacrificed, his disciples said to him, "Where do you want us to go and make the preparations for you to eat the Passover?" So he sent two of his disciples, saying to them, "Go into the city, and a man carrying a jar of water will meet you; follow him, and wherever he enters, say to the owner of the house, 'The Teacher asks, Where is my guest room where I may eat the Passover with my disciples?' He will show you a large room upstairs, furnished and ready. Make preparations for us there." So the disciples set out and went to the city, and found everything as he had told them; and they prepared the Passover meal.

When it was evening, he came with the twelve. And when they had taken their places and were eating, Jesus said, "Truly I tell you, one of you will betray me, one who is eating with me." They

began to be distressed and to say to him one after another, "Surely, not I?" He said to them, "It is one of the twelve, one who is dipping bread into the bowl with me. For the Son of Man goes as it is written of him, but woe to that one by whom the Son of Man is betrayed! It would have been better for that one not to have been born."

While they were eating, he took a loaf of bread, and after blessing it he broke it, gave it to them, and said, "Take; this is my body." Then he took a cup, and after giving thanks he gave it to them, and all of them drank from it. He said to them, "This is my blood of the covenant, which is poured out for many. Truly I tell you, I will never again drink of the fruit of the vine until that day when I drink it new in the kingdom of God."

When they had sung the hymn, they went out to the Mount of Olives. (Mark 14:12–26)

Reflect on the Mystery

This year I started going to a new school. It is a private, all-girls' Catholic high school, and it offers the opportunity to attend Mass every day. At first I didn't attend Mass every day because I felt that if I went to Mass on Sundays, why go on other days? Gradually I began to attend Mass every day. After receiving the Eucharist, I am able to feel at peace with myself and with God. Now that I am in the tradition of receiving the Eucharist on a daily basis, I find that when I miss Mass for one reason or another, I feel incomplete. The sacrament of Holy Communion has affected me in that I now depend more on God, which has improved my spiritual life. There is a saying about how you never know what you have until you are unable to access it. I never really recognized Christ in the Eucharist until I found receiving Jesus in this way was comforting but then was unable to receive it for one reason or another. I still go to Mass every day possible, but if I am unable to attend Mass, I feel a little lost for the rest of the day. (Elysha Schickel, 15, Natick, Massachusetts)

Enter the Silence

Take some time to reflect in silence on God's word and how it is speaking to you in this moment.

Intention for Prayer (optional)

Lord, I open my heart to the way in which you will reveal yourself to me through the Eucharist so that I may respond with my life. Amen.

Pray the Decade

◆ Our Father . . .

◆ Hail Mary . . . *[Repeat ten in succession.]*

◆ Glory to . . .

Concluding the Luminous Mysteries

To conclude the luminous mysteries say the following prayers:

◆ **The Doxology**

> Glory to the Father, and to the Son, and to the Holy Spirit:
> as it was in the beginning, is now, and will be for ever.
> Amen.

◆ **Hail Holy Queen** *(Salve Regina)*

> Hail, holy Queen, mother of Mercy,
> hail, our life, our sweetness, and our hope.
> To you we cry, the children of Eve;
> to you we send up our sighs,
> mourning and weeping in this land of exile.

Turn, then, most gracious advocate,
your eyes of mercy toward us;
lead us home at last
and show us the blessed fruit of your womb, Jesus:
O clement, O loving, O sweet Virgin Mary.
Turn, then, most gracious advocate,
your eyes of mercy toward us;
lead us home at last
and show us the blessed fruit of your womb, Jesus:
O clement, O loving, O sweet Virgin Mary.

You may end here or continue with these words:

Pray for us, O holy Mother of God, that we may be made worthy of the promises of Christ. Let us pray.

+ **Closing Prayer** (optional)

O God, whose only begotten Son, by his life, death, and Resurrection, has purchased for us the rewards of eternal life, grant, we beseech you, that meditating upon these mysteries of the most holy rosary of the Blessed Virgin Mary, we may imitate what they contain and obtain what they promise. Through the same Christ, our Lord. Amen. (Anne Vail, *Joy of the Rosary*, page 40)

+ **The Sign of the Cross.** "In the name of the Father, and of the Son, and of the Holy Spirit. Amen."

CHAPTER 4

The Sorrowful Mysteries

Begin the sorrowful mysteries with the following prayers:

* **The Sign of the Cross.** Hold the cross of the rosary in your right hand and make the sign of the cross: "In the name of the Father, and of the Son, and of the Holy Spirit. Amen."

* **The Apostles' Creed.** Profess the Apostles' Creed while you are holding the cross:

  I believe in God, the Father almighty,
  creator of heaven and earth.
  I believe in Jesus Christ, his only Son, our Lord.
  He was conceived by the power of the Holy Spirit
  and born of the Virgin Mary.
  He suffered under Pontius Pilate,
  was crucified, died, and was buried.
  He descended to the dead.
  On the third day he rose again.
  He ascended into heaven,
  and is seated at the right hand of the Father.
  He will come again to judge the living and the dead.

  I believe in the Holy Spirit,
  the holy catholic Church,
  the communion of saints,
  the forgiveness of sins,
  the resurrection of the body,
  and the life everlasting.
  Amen.

- **The Lord's Prayer.** Proceed to the first larger bead and pray the Lord's Prayer:

> Our Father, who art in heaven,
> hallowed be thy name;
> thy kingdom come;
> thy will be done on earth as it is in heaven.
> Give us this day our daily bread;
> and forgive us our trespasses
> as we forgive those who trespass against us;
> and lead us not into temptation,
> but deliver us from evil.
> Amen.

- **Three Hail Marys.** Pray the Hail Mary on the following three smaller beads:

> Hail Mary, full of grace,
> the Lord is with you!
> Blessed are you among women,
> and blessed is the fruit of your womb, Jesus.
> Holy Mary, Mother of God,
> pray for us sinners
> now and at the hour of our death.
> Amen.

- **The Doxology.** Conclude with the Doxology on the last larger bead of the short strand:

> Glory to the Father, and to the Son, and to the Holy Spirit:
> as it was in the beginning, is now, and will be for ever.
> Amen.

The First Sorrowful Mystery: The Agony of Jesus in the Garden

Listen to God's Word

> They went to a place called Gethsemane and he said to his disciples, "Sit here while I pray." He took with him Peter and James and John, and began to be distressed and agitated. And he

said to them, "I am deeply grieved, even to death; remain here, and keep awake." And going a little farther, he threw himself on the ground and prayed that, if it were possible, the hour might pass from him. He said, "Abba, Father, for you all things are possible; remove this cup from me; yet, not what I want, but what you want." He came and found them sleeping; and he said to Peter, "Simon, are you asleep? Could you not keep awake one hour? Keep awake and pray that you may not come into the time of trial; the spirit indeed is willing, but the flesh is weak." And again he went away and prayed, saying the same words. And once more he came and found them sleeping, for their eyes were very heavy; and they did not know what to say to him. He came a third time and said to them, "Are you still sleeping and taking your rest? Enough! The hour has come; the Son of Man is betrayed into the hands of sinners. Get up, let us be going. See, my betrayer is at hand." (Mark 14:32–42)

Reflect on the Mystery

One day at school last year, I was eating lunch at the usual table, with the usual people, at the usual lunch period, talking about the usual things when I noticed at the table next to ours a student who looked familiar. We all knew who he was, but he wasn't exactly well received by the other students because of a mental disorder he had. He was different. He always sat at his table eating his lunch and looking around for people to sit with. Everyone, of course, quickly dismissed him by saying, "Oh, this seat is taken," or "We're leaving now; sorry, David." So he would just sit there alone day after day.

For a long time I agonized over it, because I knew all along what I had to do. That popular, sometimes annoying, acronym would pop into my head: WWJD (What Would Jesus Do?). On this particular day, I got up enough nerve to go over to David and ask, "Hey, Dave, why don't you come sit with me and my friends?" He smiled a big smile, promptly stood up, and came over to my table with me. My friends did not look too happy. Some of them even stood up and left! Inside, I was asking myself, "Why am I doing this?" because this simple gesture would have its consequences. I realized afterward that I did it for a simple reason: to try and live the way Jesus did. (Christopher Gosselin, 17, Chelmsford, Massachusetts)

Enter the Silence

Take some time to reflect in silence on God's word and how it is speaking to you in this moment.

Intention for Prayer (optional)

Lord, help me to put aside my own wants and do the right thing for the good of others. Amen.

Pray the Decade

- ◆ Our Father . . .
- ◆ Hail Mary . . . *[Using the next ten beads, repeat ten in succession.]*
- ◆ Glory to . . .

The Second Sorrowful Mystery: The Scourging at the Pillar

Listen to God's Word

So Pilate, wishing to satisfy the crowd, released Barabbas for them; and after flogging Jesus, he handed him over to be crucified. (Mark 15:15)

Reflect on the Mystery

He was the shortest freshman in the school. He wasn't exactly the smartest kid either. I'll call him Fred.

During the first week of school, Fred became popular—the popular one to pick on. There was no way he could compete with others. He was small, and his friends would never be able to provide the kind of protection he needed from the intimidating older classmen. He became their new toy.

Most of the bullying would take place after school, but on this particular day, it happened before the first bell. As Fred stood by his out-of-the-way locker, attempting to organize his books and notebooks for the first round of classes, a few of the brawly, popular upperclassmen swiped Fred's backpack, tied up his hands and feet, and shoved him in his locker. The cheers and laughter resonated through the cement-block hallway, and the stares the culprits gave were stares of death, causing everyone to scatter into their homerooms. By lunchtime, the buzz about the morning's event had spread like wildfire. Interestingly, no one questioned the outcome. No one really noticed that Fred didn't attend any of his classes. As it was, Fred was left hanging in his locker the entire day. He never muttered a word, afraid he would get beat up. Fred was finally discovered by a janitor who could hear his sobbing.

Fred was just another kid, and those things happen in school all the time. What's the big deal, right? It was a good laugh. It made for a great story. It certainly made those upperclassmen feel powerful. Fred was a friend from when we were younger, and I was too afraid to stop what was happening to him for fear of losing my own popularity. I just stood by and watched. (Anonymous)

Enter the Silence

Take some time to reflect in silence on God's word and how it is speaking to you in this moment.

Intention for Prayer (optional)

Lord, forgive me for the times I have hurt someone either by what I have said or by what I have done or not done. Give me the courage to seek reconciliation not only with you but with those I have hurt. Help me to forgive as the Father forgives. Amen.

Pray the Decade

+ Our Father . . .

+ Hail Mary . . . *[Repeat ten in succession.]*

+ Glory to . . .

The Third Sorrowful Mystery: The Crowning of Thorns

Listen to God's Word

Then the soldiers led him into the courtyard of the palace (that is, the governor's headquarters); and they called together the whole cohort. And they clothed him in a purple cloak; and after twisting some thorns into a crown, they put it on him. And they began saluting him, "Hail, King of the Jews!" They struck his head with a reed, spat on him, and knelt down in homage to him. After mocking him, they stripped him of the purple cloak and put his own clothes on him. Then they led him out to crucify him. (Mark 15:16–20)

Reflect on the Mystery

Last May I ran for class president and lost. At that point in my life, I had never strived for a goal and not achieved it. Even though I lost the election for class president, I won in so many other ways.

At first, hearing the results made me think, "I just wasted a lot of money, a lot of time (my own and that of my friends and family), and a lot of effort." But now I've come to realize that maybe it wasn't a waste after all. In one month I accomplished more than I ever thought possible, and although someone else came out on top, I know that I gave it my all.

It's hard, because in the beginning, I never once had a doubt in my head or second-guessed myself. I knew I could do a great job, and that was that.

Unfortunately, after the results I felt like I had thrown myself to the dogs. I cried. I let other people see the emotional, vulnerable side of me for the first time. Until then I had always let other people cry on *my* shoulder. I was strong enough to get through things on my own. Not this time, though. I let my friends help me through it, I cried with the other candidates, and I turned to my family for support. Reaching out to others was a huge step for me; I learned that there are people all around me that I can always count on.

Never knowing exactly why I didn't get elected president is okay with me. I took a lot out of the experience, maybe more than some of the winners did. Although the experience was painful, it turned out to have a positive effect on who I am. (Faye LaRochelle, 18, Chelmsford, Massachusetts)

Enter the Silence

Take some time to reflect in silence on God's word and how it is speaking to you in this moment.

Intention for Prayer (optional)

Lord, help me to rise above the pain of being picked on, laughed at, or disappointed in myself, especially when it causes me embarrass-ment and humiliation. Amen.

Pray the Decade

◆ Our Father . . .

◆ Hail Mary . . . *[Repeat ten in succession.]*

◆ Glory to . . .

The Fourth Sorrowful Mystery: The Carrying of the Cross

Listen to God's Word

As they led him away, they seized a man, Simon of Cyrene, who was coming from the country, and they laid the cross on him,

and made him carry it behind Jesus. A great number of the people followed him, and among them were women who were beating their breasts and wailing for him. But Jesus turned to them and said, "Daughters of Jerusalem, do not weep for me, but weep for yourselves and for your children. For the days are surely coming when they will say, 'Blessed are the barren, and the wombs that never bore, and the breasts that never nursed.' Then they will begin to say to the mountains, 'Fall on us'; and to the hills, 'Cover us.' For if they do this when the wood is green, what will happen when it is dry?" (Luke 23:26–31)

Reflect on the Mystery

Two summers ago I went on a mission trip with my archdiocese to New York City. I had been on several local missions before, so I thought I was pretty pre- pared. The week got off to a great start. I helped out at a homeless shelter and at a day-care center—all the usual mission activities. On the fourth day, my group was assigned to help out at a day center that served people with mental handicaps. This scared the daylights out of me. I wanted nothing to do with this service project. On the train ride in, I was sitting in my seat shaking. I wasn't even really sure why I was scared. I think it was because I had never worked with mentally handicapped people before. When we arrived at the center, I was still very nerv- ous. There were some options, but a friend and I were assigned to work with the elderly group all day. They walked us over to their building, and the day began. At first I just sat in the front of the room; I didn't speak to anyone. Then an elderly lady named Claire asked me to help her with her writing. I took the plunge. I said okay. I sat next to her for the next two hours, talking about the weather and the beach, still struggling to teach her to write her *Ts* correctly. I almost forgot that she had a disability. The rest of the day, I helped different people with puzzles, coloring, and cooking.

This experience opened my eyes. I realized that I want nothing more than to help people with disabilities. Now, in school, I help students who have Down syndrome and cerebral palsy. I am fascinated every day that no matter how severe these students' handicaps may be, they still tell me every day that it is "the best day ever." (Christopher Gosselin, 16, Westford, Massachusetts)

Enter the Silence

Take some time to reflect in silence on God's word and how it is speaking to you in this moment.

Intention for Prayer (optional)

Lord, help me to trust you in leading me to the places and situations where you will call forth the gifts you have given me to be used for the good of others. Strengthen my trust in you, most especially when I go reluctantly or when I'm being told I have to. I'm glad you lead me to these places, because somehow I always find you there, and helping others always helps me to grow and become more like you. Help me to become more accepting of the opportunities that are good for me from the start and to trust you as much as you trust me. Amen.

Pray the Decade

- ◆ Our Father . . .

- ◆ Hail Mary . . . *[Repeat ten in succession.]*

- ◆ Glory to . . .

The Fifth Sorrowful Mystery:
The Crucifixion

Listen to God's Word

And they offered him wine mixed with myrrh; but he did not take it. And they crucified him, and divided his clothes among them, casting lots to decide what each should take.

It was nine o'clock in the morning when they crucified him. The inscription of the charge against him read, "The King of the Jews." And with him they crucified two bandits, one on his right and one on his left. Those who passed by derided him, shaking their heads and saying, "Aha! You who would destroy the temple and build it in three days, save yourself, and come down from the cross!" In the same way the chief priests, along with the scribes, were also mocking him among themselves and saying, "He saved others; he cannot save himself. Let the Messiah, the King of Israel, come down from the cross now, so that we may see and believe." Those who were crucified with him also taunted him.

When it was noon, darkness came over the whole land until three in the afternoon. At three o'clock Jesus cried out with a loud voice, "Eloi, Eloi, lema sabachthani?" which means, "My God, my God, why have you forsaken me?" When some of the bystanders heard it, they said, "Listen, he is calling for Elijah." And someone ran, filled a sponge with sour wine, put it on a stick, and gave it to him to drink, saying, "Wait, let us see whether Elijah will come to take him down." Then Jesus gave a loud cry and breathed his last. And the curtain of the temple was torn in two, from top to bottom. Now when the centurion, who stood facing him, saw that in this way he breathed his last, he said, "Truly this man was God's Son!"

There were also women looking on from a distance; among them were Mary Magdalene, and Mary the mother of James the younger and of Joses, and Salome. These used to follow him and provided for him when he was in Galilee; and there were many other women who had come up with him to Jerusalem. (Mark 15:23–41)

Reflect on the Mystery

Three years ago I learned that my great grandfather had terminal throat cancer. After a time of being sad, I learned to deal with the fact that he was going to die and there was nothing I could do. As each week passed, he got worse. Pépère Bob lived in a log cabin on a mountain in New Hampshire, where he was happiest. He spent the last few months of his life in a hospital bed in my grandmother's living room. It saddened me to see him taken away from the mountain, but he constantly wore a smile. One thing he really loved that was nearby was Chelmsford Ginger Ale. It was amazing to see how something so simple could bring him so much joy. During the last few weeks of his life, he was in a lot of pain and constantly vomiting. A tube was inserted into his stomach so he could eat. I was sad to see that the one comfort I could give him, the ginger ale, he was no longer able to enjoy. Knowing I could do nothing else, I turned to prayer and spending time with him. I know this meant a lot to him. (Andrew Adams, 15, Chelmsford, Massachusetts)

Enter the Silence

Take some time to reflect in silence on God's word and how it is speaking to you in this moment.

Intention for Prayer (optional)

Lord, give me courage, trust, patience, and understanding when there is nothing I can do but watch and pray for someone who is suffering, most especially when it is someone I know and love. Amen.

Pray the Decade

+ Our Father . . .

+ Hail Mary . . . *[Repeat ten in succession.]*

+ Glory to . . .

Concluding the Sorrowful Mysteries

To conclude the sorrowful mysteries, say the following prayers:

+ **The Doxology**

    Glory to the Father, and to the Son, and to the Holy Spirit: as it was in the beginning, is now, and will be for ever.
    Amen.

+ **Hail Holy Queen** *(Salve Regina)*

    Hail, holy Queen, mother of Mercy,
    hail, our life, our sweetness, and our hope.
    To you we cry, the children of Eve;
    to you we send up our sighs,
    mourning and weeping in this land of exile.
    Turn, then, most gracious advocate,
    your eyes of mercy toward us;
    lead us home at last
    and show us the blessed fruit of your womb,
              Jesus:
    O clement, O loving, O sweet Virgin Mary.
    Turn, then, most gracious advocate,
    your eyes of mercy toward us;
    lead us home at last
    and show us the blessed fruit of your womb,
              Jesus:
    O clement, O loving, O sweet Virgin Mary.

You may end here or continue with these words:

> Pray for us, O holy Mother of God, that we may be made worthy of the promises of Christ. Let us pray.

- **Closing Prayer** (optional)

  O God, whose only begotten Son, by his life, death, and Resurrection, has purchased for us the rewards of eternal life, grant, we beseech you, that meditating upon these mysteries of the most holy rosary of the Blessed Virgin Mary, we may imitate what they contain and obtain what they promise. Through the same Christ, our Lord. Amen. (Anne Vail, *Joy of the Rosary,* page 40)

- **The Sign of the Cross.** "In the name of the Father, and of the Son, and of the Holy Spirit. Amen."

CHAPTER 5

The Glorious Mysteries

Begin the glorious mysteries with the following prayers:

♦ **The Sign of the Cross.** Hold the cross of the rosary in your right hand and make the sign of the cross: "In the name of the Father, and of the Son, and of the Holy Spirit. Amen."

♦ **The Apostles' Creed.** Profess the Apostles' Creed while you are holding the cross:

> I believe in God, the Father almighty,
> > creator of heaven and earth.
> I believe in Jesus Christ, his only Son, our Lord.
> > He was conceived by the power of the Holy Spirit
> > > and born of the Virgin Mary.
> > He suffered under Pontius Pilate,
> > > was crucified, died, and was buried.
> > He descended to the dead.
> > On the third day he rose again.
> > He ascended into heaven,
> > > and is seated at the right hand of the Father.
> > He will come again to judge the living and the dead.
>
> I believe in the Holy Spirit,
> > the holy catholic Church,
> > the communion of saints,
> > the forgiveness of sins,
> > the resurrection of the body,
> > and the life everlasting.
> > Amen.

- ♦ **The Lord's Prayer.** Proceed to the first larger bead and pray the Lord's Prayer:

> Our Father, who art in heaven,
> hallowed be thy name;
> thy kingdom come;
> thy will be done on earth as it is in heaven.
> Give us this day our daily bread;
> and forgive us our trespasses
> as we forgive those who trespass against us;
> and lead us not into temptation,
> but deliver us from evil.
> Amen.

- ♦ **Three Hail Marys.** Pray the Hail Mary on the following three smaller beads:

> Hail Mary, full of grace,
> the Lord is with you!
> Blessed are you among women,
> and blessed is the fruit of your womb, Jesus.
> Holy Mary, Mother of God,
> pray for us sinners
> now and at the hour of our death.
> Amen.

- ♦ **The Doxology.** Conclude with the Doxology on the last larger bead of the short strand:

> Glory to the Father, and to the Son, and to the Holy Spirit:
> as it was in the beginning, is now, and will be for ever.
> Amen.

The First Glorious Mystery: The Resurrection of Jesus

Listen to God's Word

> When the sabbath was over, Mary Magdalene, and Mary the mother of James, and Salome bought spices, so that they might go and anoint him. And very early on the first day of the week,

when the sun had risen, they went to the tomb. They had been saying to one another, "Who will roll away the stone for us from the entrance to the tomb?" When they looked up, they saw that the stone, which was very large, had already been rolled back. As they entered the tomb, they saw a young man, dressed in a white robe, sitting on the right side; and they were alarmed. But he said to them, "Do not be alarmed; you are looking for Jesus of Nazareth, who was crucified. He has been raised; he is not here. Look, there is the place they laid him. But go, tell his disciples and Peter that he is going ahead of you to Galilee; there you will see him, just as he told you." So they went out and fled from the tomb, for terror and amazement had seized them; and they said nothing to anyone for they were afraid.

Now after he rose early on the first day of the week, he appeared first to Mary Magdalene, from whom he had cast out seven demons. She went out and told those who had been with him, while they were mourning and weeping. But when they heard that he was alive and had been seen by her, they would not believe it. (Mark 16:1–11)

Reflect on the Mystery

About half a year ago, I was diagnosed with clinical depression. I had been struggling for almost two years of my life, and nobody noticed. I was the type of kid who always made good grades and was involved in tons of extracurriculars. Nobody saw how empty I was inside or how sick I had become. Nobody noticed, and what's more, I didn't want them to.

Things grew increasingly worse. I began to isolate myself from everything—family, friends, and even God. I shut everything out, saying that I had too much work and no time for anything. Eventually it caught up with me, and I made a complete one-eighty. I shoved everything aside and slept all the time, whenever I could. I just didn't care about anyone or anything. At this point I was completely lost. I had no control of who I was or what I was becoming. In an effort to kill the bad in my life, I had lost all the good.

One particular night I got the crazy idea to pray. My parents figured out what was happening and sent me to a therapist, with whom I'm still working through some things. I have the feeling that God was listening to me that night and sent the help I needed, even though I didn't want it at the time. It just goes to show that prayer is a powerful thing and it should never be underestimated. You never know when or how God is going to answer your cries. (K. Gurley, 16, Lexington, Kentucky)

Enter the Silence

Take some time to reflect in silence on God's word and how it is speaking to you in this moment.

Intention for Prayer (optional)

Lord, thank you for the gift of your Son, Jesus. Because of him I can experience a joy like no other joy; I can experience life renewed, and you are always giving me that chance—the opportunity to change, to grow in your love, to forgive and be forgiven, and to experience life in you. Thank you for those times when you are so very present to me—even when no one quite understands what I'm feeling because of them. Give me the words to help others understand your power and your love. Amen.

Pray the Decade

♦ Our Father . . .

♦ Hail Mary . . . *[Using the next ten beads, repeat ten in succession.]*

♦ Glory to . . .

The Second Glorious Mystery: The Ascension of Jesus into Heaven

Listen to God's Word

So when they had come together, they asked him, "Lord, is this the time when you will restore the kingdom to Israel?" He replied, "It is not for you to know the times or periods that the Father has set by his own authority. But you will receive power when the Holy Spirit has come upon you; and you will be my witnesses in Jerusalem, in all Judea and Samaria, and to the ends of the earth." When he had said this, as they were watching, he was lifted up, and a cloud took him out of their sight. While he was going and they were gazing up toward heaven, suddenly two men in white robes stood by them. They said, "Men of Galilee, why do you stand looking up toward heaven? This Jesus, who has been taken up from you into heaven, will come in the same way as you saw him go into heaven."

Then they returned to Jerusalem from the mount called Olivet, which is near Jerusalem, a sabbath day's journey away. When they had entered the city, they went to the room upstairs where they were staying, Peter, and John, and James, and Andrew, Philip and Thomas, Bartholomew and Matthew, James son of Alphaeus, and Simon the Zealot, and Judas son of James. All these were constantly devoting themselves to prayer, together with certain women, including Mary the mother of Jesus, as well as his brothers. (Acts 1:6–14)

Reflect on the Mystery

When I was a sophomore in high school, my aunt died of a brain aneurysm. I felt my knees give way as I slumped to the ground in tears when my mother delivered the news. It was so sudden. I didn't know what to do. This woman had been a huge influence in my life. She was the model Christian. She lived her life according to the beatitudes, and there she was, dead. I remember thinking "Why, God, why? Why did you take her from me?" There was no one on earth who could answer that for me. All I could do was pray. I never got an answer in the form of a burning bush or a thundering cloud, but I came to understand that I didn't need to know why. I needed healing. My prayers changed from "Why did you do this?" to "Please help me get through this." I believe that in every "bad" situation there is good. The good is that I learned much from her death. God doesn't always give us what we want, but always takes care of us. (Carla Anne Hernandez, 18, Lancaster, California)

Enter the Silence

Take some time to reflect in silence on God's word and how it is speaking to you in this moment.

Intention for Prayer (optional)

Lord, I ask for the patience to wait for your response and action, especially when I want it immediately. Teach me to pray, and pray with me in those moments. Help me to trust that you know what is best for me. Amen.

Pray the Decade

◆ Our Father . . .

◆ Hail Mary . . . *[Repeat ten in succession.]*

◆ Glory to . . .

The Third Glorious Mystery: The Descent of the Holy Spirit on the Apostles (Pentecost)

Listen to God's Word

When the day of Pentecost had come, they were all together in one place. And suddenly from heaven there came a sound like the rush of a violent wind, and it filled the entire house where they were sitting. Divided tongues, as of fire, appeared among them, and a tongue rested on each of them. All of them were filled with the Holy Spirit and began to speak in other languages, as the Spirit gave them ability.

Now there were devout Jews from every nation under heaven living in Jerusalem. And at this sound the crowd gathered and was bewildered, because each one heard them speaking in the native language of each. Amazed and astonished, they asked, "Are not all these who are speaking Galileans? And how is it that we hear, each of us, in our own native language? Parthians, Medes, Elamites, and residents of Mesopotamia, Judea and Cappadocia, Pontus and Asia, Phrygia and Pamphylia, Egypt and the parts of Libya belonging to Cyrene, and visitors from Rome, both Jews and proselytes, Cretans and Arabs—in our own languages we hear them speaking about God's deeds of power." All were amazed and perplexed, saying to one another, "What does this mean?" But others sneered and said, "They are filled with new wine."

But Peter, standing with the eleven, raised his voice and addressed them, "Men of Judea and all who live in Jerusalem, let this be known to you, and listen to what I say. Indeed, these are not drunk, as you suppose, for it is only nine o'clock in the morning. No, this is what was spoken through the prophet Joel:
'In the last days it will be, God declares,
   that I will pour out my Spirit upon all flesh,
      and your sons and your daughters shall prophesy,
   and your young men shall see visions,
      and your old men shall dream dreams.

Even upon my slaves, both men and women,
   in those days I will pour out my Spirit;
     and they shall prophesy.
And I will show portents in the heaven above
   and signs on the earth below,
     blood, and fire, and smoky mist.
The sun shall be turned to darkness
   and the moon to blood,
     before the coming of the Lord's great and
      glorious day.
Then everyone who calls on the name of the Lord shall
     be saved.'"

(Acts 2:1–21)

Reflect on the Mystery

I went on a mission trip to West Virginia the summer before my junior year of high school. It was a typical trip, as far as mission trips go. The one event that sticks out is a particular prayer session the group had. All of us were sitting in a circle in a classroom of the old elementary school where we were staying. The adult leaders of our individual groups were kneeling before us and washing our feet, just as Jesus did for his disciples. After they finished, everyone was still; quiet. Then, all at once, everyone stood up and started embracing each other (those we knew and even those we did not know!). There were people crying, both guys and girls! It was a truly moving moment; one in which I know the Holy Spirit was present and alive in that room and in each of us. I will never forget it. (Hannah (Corey) Beaver, 18, New Salisbury, Indiana)

Enter the Silence

Take some time to reflect in silence on God's word and how it is speaking to you in this moment.

Intention for Prayer (optional)

Come, Holy Spirit, and fill my life with your unconditional love, your comforting peace, and your
transforming fire, creating me and the world anew.
Help me to trust in the gifts you give so freely, to
share and receive them, for the life of the world.
Amen.

Pray the Decade

- ◆ Our Father . . .
- ◆ Hail Mary . . . *[Repeat ten in succession.]*
- ◆ Glory to . . .

The Fourth Glorious Mystery:
The Assumption of Mary into Heaven

Listen to God's Word

My beloved speaks and says to me:
"Arise, my love, my fair one,
    and come away;
for now the winter is past,
    the rain is over and gone.
The flowers appear on the earth;
    the time of singing has come,
and the voice of the turtledove
    is heard in our land.
The fig tree puts forth its figs,
    and the vines are in blossom;
    they give forth fragrance.
Arise, my love, my fair one,
    and come away."

.   .   .   .

Come with me from Lebanon, my bride;
    come with me from Lebanon.
Depart from the peak of Amana,
    from the peak of Senir and Hermon,
from the dens of lions,
    from the mountains of leopards.
You have ravished my heart, my sister, my bride,
    you have ravished my heart with a glance of your eyes,
    with one jewel of your necklace.
how sweet is your love, my sister, my bride!
    How much better is your love than wine,
    and the fragrance of your oils than any spice!

(Song of Solomon 2:10–13, 4:8–10)

Reflect on the Mystery

I have been going to the same church every Sunday since the day I was two years old. Some people find comfort in this type of regularity, but I began to feel the weight of such a routine when I entered my early teens. The same hymns, the same preachers, the same parishioners, and the same homilies transformed what should have been a faith experience into a well-deserved naptime at the end of an exhausting weekend. One Sunday, an early-morning brunch conflicted with my family's normal routine, and I found myself attending the five o'clock Life Teen Mass, which is led by and directed toward teens. In that one hour and fifteen minutes, my interaction with God was reinstated. The music, the people, and the message all came together that night to make me realize what my faith was all about: me and God. Jesus became a person to whom I could relate; more than that, he became my best friend. By uniting with Jesus, a previously distant figure, I came to fully realize his true and overwhelming love for me and for all creation. (Carolyn Pippen, 16, Lexington, Kentucky)

Enter the Silence

Take some time to reflect in silence on God's word and how it is speaking to you in this moment.

Intention for Prayer (optional)

Lord, take my heart; take my life and unite it to yours. I want to feel close to you. Amen.

Pray the Decade

- ◆ Our Father . . .
- ◆ Hail Mary . . . *[Repeat ten in succession.]*
- ◆ Glory to . . .

The Fifth Glorious Mystery: The Crowning of Mary as Queen of Heaven

Listen to God's Word

A great portent appeared in heaven: a woman clothed with the sun, with the moon under her feet, and on her head a crown of twelve stars. She was pregnant and was crying out in birth pangs, in the agony of giving birth. Then another portent appeared in heaven: a great red dragon, with seven heads and ten horns, and seven diadems on his heads. His tail swept down a third of the stars of heaven and threw them to the earth. Then the dragon stood before the woman who was about to bear a child, so that he might devour her child as soon as it was born. And she gave birth to a son, a male child, who is to rule all nations with a rod of iron. But her child was snatched away and taken to God and to his throne; and the woman fled into the wilderness, where she has a place prepared by God, so that there she can be nourished for one thousand two hundred sixty days.

And war broke out in heaven; Michael and his angels fought against the dragon. The dragon and his angels fought back, but they were defeated, and there was no longer any place for them in heaven. The great dragon was thrown down, that ancient serpent, who is called the Devil and Satan, the deceiver of the whole world—he was thrown down to the earth, and his angels were thrown down with him.

Then I heard a loud voice in heaven, proclaiming,
"Now have come the salvation and the power
    and the kingdom of our God
    and the authority of his Messiah,
for the accuser of our comrades has been thrown down,
    who accuses them day and night before our God.
But they have conquered him by the blood of the Lamb
    and by the word of their testimony,
for they did not cling to life even in the face of death.
Rejoice then, you heavens
    and those who dwell in them!
But woe to the earth and the sea,
    for the devil has come down to you
with great wrath,
    because he knows that his time is short!"

So when the dragon saw that he had been thrown down to the earth, he pursued the woman who had given birth to the male child. But the woman was given the two wings of the great eagle, so that she could fly from the serpent into the wilderness, to her place where she is nourished for a time, and times, and half a time. Then from his mouth the serpent poured water like a river after the woman, to sweep her away with the flood. But the earth came to the help of the woman; it opened its mouth and swallowed the river that the dragon had poured from his mouth. Then the dragon was angry with the woman, and went off to make war on the rest of her children, those who keep the commandments of God and hold the testimony of Jesus. (Revelation 12:1–17)

Reflect on the Mystery

I have ridden horses ever since I can remember. The pony Rainbows was my partner at shows. She and I endured grueling training sessions, many successes, and a few defeats. When I was twelve, Rainbows injured a tendon. During her convalescence she developed a disease of the hoof known as founder. She had an allergic reaction to the anti-inflammatory medication she was given, which made her kidneys shut down. Rainbows grew weaker and weaker. One day, as Mom and I were standing by her field, she said, "I think Rainbows is going to die." We both already knew this, but when she said it, we hugged each other and cried. Soon after this, as we were leaving home, Rainbows collapsed in front of the barn. We were all horrified, and before we left, I went to Rainbows and kissed her goodbye. As we pulled away, I looked in the rearview mirror of the car and saw my little chestnut pony lying flat on her side. She looked so thin and tired. I knew as we pulled away that I wouldn't see Rainbows again. As we left, Mom took my hand in hers and squeezed it. The death of my beloved pony could have been the end of my riding career. However, my mom supported and cared for me through that painful time. She helped me put Rainbows' death behind me and start anew with another show partner. (Virginia Deaton, 16, Salvisa, Kentucky)

Enter the Silence

Take some time to reflect in silence on God's word and how it is speaking to you in this moment.

Intention for Prayer (optional)

Mary, help me grow in faith, just as you helped Jesus grow in faith when he was a teenager. Pray for me, and help me understand Jesus as you do. Lord Jesus, thank you for the gift of Mary, who is mother to us both and who trusted God completely. May I come to learn from her and to experience her love and care for me, just as you experienced it when you were growing up. Amen.

Pray the Decade

♦ Our Father . . .

♦ Hail Mary . . . *[Repeat ten in succession.]*

♦ Glory to . . .

Concluding the Glorious Mysteries

To conclude the glorious mysteries, ssay the following prayers:

♦ **The Doxology**

> Glory to the Father, and to the Son, and to the Holy Spirit: as it was in the beginning, is now, and will be for ever. Amen.

♦ **Hail Holy Queen** *(Salve Regina)*

> Hail, holy Queen, mother of Mercy,
> hail, our life, our sweetness, and our hope.
> To you we cry, the children of Eve;
> to you we send up our sighs,
> mourning and weeping in this land of exile.
> Turn, then, most gracious advocate,
> your eyes of mercy toward us;
> lead us home at last
> and show us the blessed fruit of your womb, Jesus:
> O clement, O loving, O sweet Virgin Mary.
> Turn, then, most gracious advocate,
> your eyes of mercy toward us;
> lead us home at last
> and show us the blessed fruit of your womb, Jesus:
> O clement, O loving, O sweet Virgin Mary.

You may end here or continue with these words:

> Pray for us, O holy Mother of God, that we may be made worthy of the promises of Christ. Let us pray.

♦ **Closing Prayer** (optional)

> O God, whose only begotten Son, by his life, death, and Resurrection, has purchased for us the rewards of eternal life, grant, we beseech you, that meditating upon these mysteries of the most holy rosary of the Blessed Virgin Mary, we may imitate what they contain and obtain what they promise. Through the same Christ, our Lord. Amen. (Anne Vail, *Joy of the Rosary,* page 40)

♦ **The Sign of the Cross.** "In the name of the Father, and of the Son, and of the Holy Spirit. Amen."

Acknowledgments

All scriptural quotations in this book are from the New Revised Standard Version of the Bible, Catholic Edition. Copyright © 1993 and 1989 by the Division of Christian Education of the National Council of the Churches of Christ in the United States of America. All rights reserved.

The quotations in this book marked *The Catholic Faith Handbook for Youth* or *CFH* are from *The Catholic Faith Handbook for Youth,* by Brian Singer-Towns et al. (Winona, MN: Saint Mary's Press, 2004). Copyright © 2004 by Saint Mary's Press. All rights reserved.

The excerpts and quotations in this book marked *Rosarium Virginis Mariae* or *RVM* are from the apostolic letter *Rosarium Virginis Mariae,* by Pope John Paul II, 2002, at *www.vatican.va/holy_father/john_paul_ii/ apost_letters/documents/hf_jp-ii_apl_20021016_rosarium-virginis-mariae _en.html,* accessed December 14, 2004.

The excerpt on page 12 is from *Praying by Hand: Rediscovering the Rosary as a Way of Prayer,* by M. Basil Pennington (New York: HarperSanFrancisco, 1991), page 33. Copyright © 1991 by the Cistercian Abbey of Spencer, Inc.

The prayers on pages 20–22, 32–33, 45, 46–47, 57–58, 59–60, 70–71, 72–73, and 85–86 are from *Catholic Household Blessings and Prayers,* by the Bishops' Committee on the Liturgy (Washington, DC: United States Conference of Catholic Bishops, Inc. [USCCB], 1989), pages 24, 375–376, 21, 38, 25, and 94, respectively. Copyright © 1989 by the USCCB. All rights reserved.

The closing prayer on pages 22, 45, 58, 71, and 86 is from *Joy of the Rosary: A Way into Meditative Prayer,* by Anne Vail (Liguori, MO: Liguori Publications, 1998), page 40. Copyright © 1997 by Anne Vail. Used with permission of Liguori Publications, Liguori, MO 63057-9999, 800-325-9521. No other reproduction or use of this material is permitted.

The illustration of the rosary on page 17 is from *Handbook for Today's Catholic,* by John Cardinal O'Conner (Liguori, MO: Liguori Publications, 1994), page 67, Copyright © 1994 by Liguori Publications. Used with permission.

Endnotes Cited in Quotations from *Rosarium Virginis Mariae*

1. Angelus: *Insegnamenti di Giovanni Paolo II,* I (1978): 75–76.

2. *I Quindici Sabati del Santissimo Rosario,* 27th ed., Pompei, 1916, 27.